Mom's Guide
to Being a
SUPERHERO

Mom's Guide to Being a
SUPERHERO

✳ Prevent bad dreams

✳ Fix plastic toys

✳ Build the best paper airplane

More than 150 ways to amaze kids

Susan Dazzo

FAIR WINDS
PRESS
GLOUCESTER, MASSACHUSETTS

Text © 2005 by Fair Winds Press

First published in the USA in 2005 by
Fair Winds Press
33 Commercial Street
Gloucester, MA 01930

08 07 06 05 04   1 2 3 4 5

ISBN 1-59233-116-5

Library of Congress Cataloging-in-Publication Data available

Cover and book design by Susan Dazzo
Cover illustration by Pamela Hobbs

Printed and bound in Canada

To Nick, Richard, Anita, and John,
for teaching me so much.
Thank you for being so patient and for loving me
even when I'm not.

❤

Contents

INSIDE SKILLS

OUTSIDE ACTIVITIES

RECIPES

Introduction

A superhero mom is the last thing I would think to call myself, and most people who know me would surely agree. Being at home caring for my kids doesn't come naturally to me. I worked full time up until the month before my third child, John, was born. (I took four- and six-month maternity leaves with the other two.) Then I decided to quit my job to be home with them.

Of course, being home more didn't mean I had more time to enjoy the kids. I was trying to do housework and childcare and found myself turning the television on too often and yelling too much. There was so much to do: laundry, cooking, straightening up ... I was frustrated with the long days, and yet I was unable to accomplish anything to completion. Forget about tackling any fun "projects" with the kids.

I soon discovered that, unlike cooking and keeping house, stimulating entertainment for the kids was absolutely necessary for everyone's sanity. Not entertainment that involved spending a lot of money and taking three kids on a field trip. I mean things we could primarily do at home, with items we had in the house or that I could easily and inexpensively find at yard sales or dollar stores.

My creativity was the one aspect of my career that I could apply to being home with the kids. Somehow my management skills didn't translate as well. I've always been impressed by mothers who can harness the energy of their children seemingly without much effort. For me, it is hard work. I've been blessed with some very energetic and highly opinionated kids.

MY FAMILIES

Richard, at seven, is the oldest of my children. He is really bright and extremely social and has an endless well of energy. One trait he inherited from my husband is his curiosity. He wants to know how everything works, and then he wants to make his own. He loves to build. His interest in learning more has been the impetus for many of the projects in this book, as you'll soon see.

Anita, four years old, has a tremendously warm and playful personality. Nick, my husband, often says to her, "You have so much love to give," and she does. She is creative and likes to sing and dance. She loves to play with her dress-up clothes especially jewelry, pocketbooks, and shoes; she is fascinated with shoes. Yet, a neighbor once described her as a tomboy. I guess because she's tough and equally comfortable playing games with the boys on the block.

John is just over two years old. I think this is the age I appreciate most, when kids are still small and cuddly but developing some independence. John often wants to "do it myself," but at the same time I can hold and cuddle him and he loves it. John has a great sense of humor. He loves to play with trains, blocks or balls. He can throw and kick exceptionally well for his age. He is charming and adorable, and like his brother and sister, a very social child.

I grew up with four brothers and three sisters, the seventh of eight children. My dad worked days and evenings at two local jobs although he always came home for dinner and sometimes for lunch. My mom did not have a "job." She obviously had her hands full working at home. I've always felt having a big family was lots of fun. But the sacrifice my parents made left a bigger impression on me. Particularly my mother, who was home with us day in and day out. My father worked hard to be sure, but he was working with responsive, potty-trained adults. Even then I thought that going out to work seemed to be more gratifying. From the time I was in high school I planned on being a career woman; marriage and children happened along the way. So, along with my career as a writer and an art director, I have three fabulous kids (and fifteen nieces and nephews).

SO WHAT IS A SUPERHERO MOM?

It often doesn't take much for your kids to think you're a hero. They get hurt and want to feel better, so you give them a boo-boo bunny, a hug, and a band-aid and you've rescued them. They want to know how to make a paper airplane so you take the time to show them, and you've done it again. You show them how to catch fireflies, and once again, you're their hero. It's not about the time or money you spend as much as it is about the quality of that time. The trick of course, is knowing the answers to their question so that you do appear to know everything: how do you keep tadpoles so you can watch them turn into frogs, anyway? How do you make a crown of flowers? How can you make a Batman action figure? You need to be resourceful. Every woman has different strengths, different goals, and different resources. It's the ways you show your children you love them that makes you a superhero. If you are true to them and true to yourself you are a superhero.

SUPERHERO MOMS ARE EVERYWHERE

This has been an important lesson for me. I've read lots of books and lots of magazine articles about the best way to approach parenting issues. But one of my best resources has been other mothers. There are so many places and situations where you can learn a skill, a fun project, or even a tip to help you get through a sticky situation with the kids. Whether it's a way to pass time quietly or to avoid a tantrum. It could be something you say or something you have your kids do. You can learn these things by observing complete strangers or by exchanging experiences with other parents. Of course, different people have different styles. You need to recognize what works for you and your children.

For this book, I have gotten inspiration from various sources. Some things I've learned during the development of the book. And some things are from lessons learned over the years that I've incorporated into my own life. I have learned to save things that might be useful for a project. For instance, I always make sure I have some egg cartons, coffee cans, toilet paper and paper towel tubes put aside. In addition, my kids and I are now exposed to many more places and people that spark ideas. We are inspired from projects we see in their classrooms, from their friends, their explorations, their books and from shows they see on television.

Parenting is hard work. As my sister-in-law Mary once said to me, "It doesn't get any easier; it just gets different." But, this book is for the fun part of parenting. It's a relatively small collection of skills, games, and crafts based on the interests of me and my kids and slanted by the things that are nostalgic to me. I hope you and your children find them entertaining.

Here's a silly skill I learned just recently from my son Richard, how to make a back scratcher. He learned it from one of his classmates. All you need is aluminum foil.

1. Rip off a piece of aluminum foil about 18 inches long.
2. Tightly scrunch it up into a long stick.
3. Put it down the back of your shirt and scratch away.

Start a Dress-up Box

I started a collection of dress-up clothes when Richard was about two. He was fascinated with Thomas the Tank Engine, so I bought him the Thomas dress-up kit. But the best suggestions I've heard for creating a dress-up box came from my friend Donna, who has two boys with very vivid imaginations and, I predict, a future in theater.

1 Shop at yard sales for real things: old ties, hats, purses, wigs, dresses, jewelry, shoes, etc. (You may even buy someone's old dress-up collection, as I did recently.)

2 Shop for costumes after Halloween. You can get the costumes and the paraphernalia at a significant savings.

3 Ask older relatives for old clothes. We have a young friend who had a thing for vests for a while. No one wears those anymore, but his stepfather had a bunch of them.

2

Stop Bad Dreams

When Richard began having bad dreams that kept him up at night I gave him a small dream catcher to keep in his room. A dream catcher allows only good dreams to pass through; bad dreams get caught in its web. He continued to have bad dreams so we decided that his dreams required a bigger dream catcher, and we got to work.

figure 1

figure 2

WHAT YOU'LL NEED
wire coat hanger
a few beads
string
a few feathers

1 Open the triangle shape of the hanger and form it into a circle. Leave the hook part intact.

2 Have your beads handy, so you can thread them onto the string at any point in the string-tying process. Tie the string to the hanger at the top of the circle. Tie it at several points around the circle, leaving loose loops between each point, then tie the end at the top, figure 1.

3 Tie a shorter piece of string at the center of the first loop. Thread it through each loop, then go back around and tie it at the starting point so you have a multi-pointed star with a circle in the middle, figure 2.

4 Repeat steps 2 and 3 within the circle of string you have created, figure 3.

5 Use the string to tie on the feathers so they hang from the frame.

6 Use the hook to hang the dream catcher in the window.

figure 3

3

Make Rainbow Crayons

Recently, my brother commented that he couldn't understand why there were always new crayons littering his house. Why buy new ones when you still have the old ones?, he wondered. Well I can tell you that new ones are so much more satisfying to color with. The sharp points help you color more neatly, and fresh crayon just goes on the paper more smoothly. But what to do with all those old ones? Melting them into rainbow-colored crayons is a fun way to give them a new life.

WHAT YOU'LL NEED
old crayons
a small muffin tin
an oven

1 Preheat the oven to 250°F.

2 Remove the paper from the crayons and break them into ¼-inch pieces.

3 Think about the color combinations you want (red, white, and blue; shades of green; sunset colors; rainbow; etc.), and arrange the crayons in a small muffin tin.

4 Place the tin in the oven for 6-9 minutes, until the crayons have begun to melt but still have some chunks.

5 Let them cool completely before removing them from the tin.

6 Cooling them in the refrigerator will make them easier to remove.

Build a House of Cards

I t got to the point where I would hide the playing cards. Richard would see them and want to build a house of cards. It was fun at first; we'd get pretty far, but then the whole thing would collapse, like a house of cards. This was terribly frustrating for Richard, and so for me. Then one day I saw a deck specifically for building houses. Each card has six slits so you can lock them into place. We needed this! But we didn't need another deck of cards in the house. Instead, I went home and got out the scissors and began to cut.

Cut a ½-inch slit at the center of each short side and two ½-inch slits on each long side of the card, about ¾ inch from the ends. For the best results, make the cuts in the same place on all the cards.

SUPER TIP

Buy some felt, 1 foot to 1 yard, in a few basic colors, just to have available. Keep it, along with some fabric scraps from old pants or shirts to use for crafts.

—KATHY, MOM OF JACK AND TOMMY

Make a Drum

In the cabinet under my kitchen sink is an empty 3-pound coffee can and a small wooden spoon. When I'm making dinner and John is clinging to my legs, I take out the can and he bangs on it while I make dinner. It makes a great drum and requires no work.

If your child is older and wants to march with his drum, you can put a couple of holes in the can and thread a rope through for a shoulder strap. Different containers will work and produce different sounds. Try using a metal or plastic coffee can, a cylindrical oatmeal container, or a powdered formula can. For drumsticks, use chopsticks or unsharpened pencils (both the eraser end and the wooden end work well).

SUPER TIP

If you have a walk-in closet, let them go into the closet and then open the door suddenly and roar loudly, pretending to be a monster or a dragon.

—DONNA, MOM OF JAMES

Press Flowers (or leaves)

The best flowers to press are delicate to begin with, such as lilies of the valley, Queen Anne's lace, pansies, bleeding hearts, violets, impatiens, and petunias. Flowers such as roses and peonies are too thick and bulky. In those cases, individual petals can be pressed. With leaves, choose ones that have good color but aren't yet brittle.

WHAT YOU'LL NEED
some big heavy books
cut flowers or leaves
newspaper
paper towel
decorative paper

1 Collect flowers or leaves one afternoon after the dew has dried. Cut the flower stems long and place them in water to keep them alive until you're ready to press.

2 Inside a big book, such as a telephone book or a dictionary, place a piece of newspaper, then a paper towel.

3 Now cut the flowers away from the stem as close to the base of the flower as possible. Arrange the flowers or leaves on the paper towel. Cover with another paper towel, then another sheet of newspaper.

4 Carefully close the book without disturbing the arrangement.

5 Place the book in a spot that is not damp, and stack more books or heavy objects on top. Leave undisturbed for one to four weeks.

6 Glue them in a pattern on decorative paper. Or make a suncatcher, see p. 188.

Make a Guitar

I think you may be surprised, as I was, at how good a sound you can get from this simple project. If you don't care what it looks like, simply take the lid off the box, place the rubber bands around the length of the box, and slip the pencil under the rubber bands across the width of the box. To make it look more like a guitar follow these steps.

WHAT YOU'LL NEED
a shoebox
scissors
2-4 rubber bands
two unsharpened pencils
a paper towel tube (optional)
tape

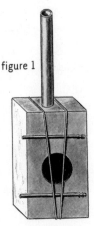

figure 1

1 Keep the lid on the box. Cut a hole in the top of the box about 3 to 4 inches in diameter.

2 Cut a hole the width of a paper towel tube in one end of the box.

3 Slide the paper towel tube into the hole and tape it in place.

4 Have your child decorate the guitar.

5 Wrap the rubber bands around the length of the box. Slip the pencils under the rubber bands on each side of the hole, figure 1.

8

Make a Mystery Box

Mystery boxes are a great way to talk to your children about the senses. Explain to them that we experience or learn about what's around us by using all of our sense (sight, touch, hearing, smell, and taste). We can take away four of our five senses and only use one-in this case, touch-to learn more about how that sense works. You can do variations on this game by blindfolding a child and having them smell or taste something, too.

Get a big cardboard box and cut two holes big enough for kids' arms to go through (and their hands). Go around the house and pick out some small recognizable objects, such as socks, balls, action figures, toy airplanes, etc., and put them into the box.

Now, have your kids put their hands into the box and tell you what they feel. You can also do this on Halloween with things that feel disgusting, such as gelatin, pudding, shaving cream, and peeled grapes (tell them they are eyeballs).

Make Play Money

Rather than give give your kids real money to play with, take out green construction paper and made fake bills. You can make each kid's bills a different color. I wrote the denomination with letters on one side and with a number on the other. You could decorate the money further if you want. One sheet of construction paper makes twelve 4 ½ x 2-inch bills.

✱ They use the money when we play shopping: we take out some groceries: cereal, rice, small canned goods, toilet paper, tissues, etc.—things that aren't perishable and won't break or crush easily. We make stacks around the living room. The shopper collects his items and brings them to the cashier. We have a very simple toy register for this. The cashier rings up the items, bags them, and tells the shopper what he owes. The shopper pays with the bills.

✱ To play train and airplane we use play tickets along with the money. Instead of a denomination I wrote "ticket" on the paper. We also save my husband's old monthly train passes and use those for tickets. We either all sit in a row on the couch or line up chairs and stools. The person who is the pilot or engineer sells and collects the tickets and sits in front to drive. The passengers bring their luggage (clothes, blankets, pillows, books) aboard and we travel (usually to wherever my husband happens to be on a business trip).

Make a Puppet Theater

This is so simple I wish I'd heard about it before I spent twenty-five bucks on a difficult-to-assemble nylon structure. It takes up too much space in my small house, but I don't want to take it apart because I know I'll never want to put it together again. So before you go out and buy a puppet theater, try making one.

Take an old curtain, sheet, or tablecloth and drape it across the bottom half of a doorway. If you don't want to tape anything to your walls, you can prop a broom handle on two chairs across the doorway and hang the fabric over that. The benefit of the doorway is that two rooms allows for a "backstage" area.

The kids crouch behind the "stage," and the audience watches from the other side.

SUPER TIP

Let your kids play with your utensils (nothing sharp, of course).
Kids love potato mashers and whisks.
Give them a pot too and they can make "soup."

—JANE, MOM OF BRENDAN AND JOSEPH

Design Jewelry

My daughter Anita loves to play with jewelry. One day when we were tracing our hands, I suggested she create jewelry for her tracings. She loved this idea and had lots of fun first designing the jewelry on paper and then cutting and gluing it to wear.

WHAT YOU'LL NEED
construction paper
markers or crayons
glue
fabric or felt, beads, buttons, or fake gemstones
string

1 Place forearms and hands with fingers open on a piece of construction paper. Trace around them with markers.

2 Younger children can draw rings and bracelets on the construction paper hands and wrists. They (or you) can cut shapes from paper and fabric and glue those on as well.

3 Older children can get more involved and thread buttons, beads, and gemstones onto string to make the jewelry more three dimensional. (Beads, buttons, and gemstones are a choking hazard for young children.)

12

Grow Potato Roots

This is a very simple science experiment that goes a long way in entertainment value. These types of activities, which invite kids to learn more about the world around them, really help make learning fun. You can also do this type of experiment with an avocado pit.

WHAT YOU'LL NEED
a potato
a glass of water
three toothpicks

1 Stick three toothpicks around the midsection of a potato.

2 Suspend the potato in a glass of water, with the toothpicks resting on the rim of the glass, so the bottom half of the potato is in the water.

3 Let it sit for one to three weeks and observe the growth of roots and shoots. Change the water if it begins to get dirty.

13

Super-Cool Karate Moves

My friend Donna has a son who loves to do karate, even at the age of three. So she asked two black belts she knows what to teach him so he wouldn't hurt anyone or himself. It's important to explain that karate is dangerous and that real karate experts do not try to make contact when they fight. Instead, they practice next to each other without making contact. There is one move that allows contact, and that's hand slaps (see below). The key is not to do what you see on TV or in the movies. Instead, tell your kid that you're going to teach her real karate. Here are three moves:

FRONT AND BACK KICKS

Stand with your feet parallel to each other and your knees slightly bent. Put up your hands as if you're boxing. Now, bring one bent knee up and then straighten your leg to the front, figure 1, or back, figure 2. This will be tough, because balancing on one leg is hard for most kids. They can hold onto a chair for balance.

HAND SLAPS

This isn't really karate-based, but it's good for kids who want contact. Put your hands out, palms facing up. Have your child put his hands on top of yours, but lightly, almost just above your palms (his palms should be facing yours).

Quickly flip your hands over his hands, so that you lightly slap the tops of his hands with your palms. While you're doing this, he should be trying to pull his hands away. If you slap his hands (gently!) then you get to go again. If he gets his hands away, it's his turn.

figure 1

ELBOW STRIKES

This is a cool move that those TV guys use. Stand with your feet parallel to each other and your knees slightly bent. With your hands up boxer-style (fists closed), bring your elbow up and out to the side, figure 3, as if you're going to elbow someone in the face. Do the same thing on the other side.

figure 2

Donna also uses her kick-boxing exercise videos with her son. This way, she gets a workout and he thinks he's learning to fight.

figure 3

Percussion Instruments

There are a bunch of simple ways to make percussion instruments. Remember, as far as your kids are concerned, the noisier, the better.

* Clean a plastic prescription medicine bottle or a film canister, and fill it with dried beans, beads, rice, or unpopped popcorn kernels. Tape the top shut. Decorate the canister by wrapping a piece of colored construction paper around it.

* Similarly, fill a plastic Easter egg and tape it shut. Fill a few with different things for different sounds.

* For a more traditional maraca, try what Richard learned at camp: maracas made from tennis balls. Cut a large slit in the balls, place beads inside, and stick a branch in the hole. Wrap fabric around the ball and secure it to the branch with an elastic band.

* Two wooden blocks or two wooden sticks (unsharpened pencils, wooden spoons) banged together make a good sound.

* Attach sandpaper to two blocks of wood and rub them together for another good sound.

* Puncture baby food or juice bottle tops and attach them to your fingers with twist ties or elastic bands to make castanets.

Color Carnations

The first time I saw this, I was shocked to learn that flowers didn't actually grow green for Saint Patrick's Day and turquoise for Easter. You can make this activity work for any holiday—red for Valentine's Day and Christmas and blue (with red and white) for The Fourth of July. Or, you can do a mix of colors for someone's birthday.

WHAT YOU'LL NEED
white carnations
water
food coloring
a clear vase or jar

1 Put some water in the vase or jar and add food coloring so the color is vibrant. Cut the base of the stem off a white carnation and place it in the water.

2 After a few hours see how the flower has changed. Keep checking; it could take up to twenty-four hours to see the results.

16

Make a Growth Chart

Don't most homes have at least one wall with pencil marks on it showing the staggering heights of the children who live there? This is one way to keep that record with you forever. I recommend making one of these for each of the children in your house.

WHAT YOU'LL NEED
a large sheet of craft paper
scissors
pencil
a thick markers and crayons
a ruler
tape

1 First, get a piece of brown paper, the kind used to wrap packages sent via mail. Cut a piece about 4 feet long.

2 Work first in pencil, then finish with a thick marker. Write your child's name boldly across the top 6 inches of the paper and decorate the top if you want with stickers or drawings.

3 Draw a line down the center of the paper, starting 7 inches from the top.

4 Hang the chart on the back of a door so the bottom edge is exactly 21 inches from the floor. Measure 3 inches up from the bottom edge and make a 2-foot mark. Measure 1 foot from there and make a 3-foot mark; another foot up make a 4-foot mark. Measure and mark off the inches in between.

5 Have our child stand with her back to the chart. Mark her height, the date, and her age. Glue or tape a recent photo near the measurement and write a caption.

6 Each time you measure her, put a photo and a caption on the chart.

7 You can use milestones as reminders to measure her. If she loses a tooth, put it in an envelope and tape it on near her height.

8 Attach drawings you think are special and measure her at the same time.

9 Attach photos of friends, pets, or special occasions and measure her at that time.

10 Decorate the chart with hand- or footprints when you measure her.

You'll end up with a growth chart that tells more than size—it will tell a story.

SUPER TIP

Make up stories about places you pass when you take walks.
Such as the magic rock or a haunted mountain.
It is a great way to help kids develop their own imagination
and storytelling techniques.

—JOAN, "MOM" TO MANY

17

Silhouette Portraits

Many amusement parks have artists making silhouettes for visitors and they can cost upwards of ten or twenty dollars. Why spend the money, though, when you can amaze your kids at home? Don't forget to let them make one of you and your husband, too.

WHAT YOU'LL NEED
white paper and a dark color paper
tape
a lamp
a pencil
scissors
glue

1 Tape a piece of white paper to the wall. Have your child sit in profile next to the wall. Place a lamp in front of her. Adjust the position of the lamp and the child until the profile is life-size and not distorted.

2 Trace the shadow onto the paper and cut it out. Glue the white paper to a nice dark color for the best effect.

Forts on the Sofa

I n a pinch, when it's been raining outside and the TV has been on too long or if the kids are bored and I need to make dinner, they can make a fort in the living room with the cushions and pillow from all of the furniture in the house—this is fun because they are making a constructive mess.

* They gather all the pillows and throw blankets from throughout the house into the living room. Then they take the seat cushions off the chairs and the couch.

* The large seat cushions go in front of the couch standing up. The other pillows act as support.

* Drape the blankets or towels over the back of the sofa and across to the cushions that are resting on the floor. The blankets make a roof.

* You can also just put furniture around the couch and drape the blankets from the couch to the furniture. Or you can use dining room chairs and drape blankets across those.

* Make sure you have a flashlight around for them to bring into the fort. They'll also want to bring in some toys and maybe some books, too.

19

Gum-Wrapper Necklace

I t seems that gum now comes in a larger variety of shapes and sizes than it used to, so you'll need to chew, or at least buy, the traditional long sticks of gum. Purchase a variety flavors to make your chain more colorful. (The wrappers from PEZ candy also work.) Save the inside foil from the gum wrappers and you can make silver jewelry. Don't mix different wrappers for one chain or it won't work.

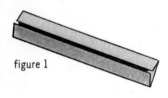
figure 1

figure 2

1 Carefully remove the wrappers from the gum. Once you have collected a number of wrappers, you can begin your chain.

2 Fold each of the wrappers in half lengthwise, then tear or cut along the fold.

3 Fold each half in half lengthwise again. Open, and then fold in each edge to meet at the crease, figure 1. Fold in half along the crease so you have a long narrow strip.

4 Fold the strip in half, bringing the two ends of the strip together.

5 Unfold, and then fold the ends so they meet at the crease, figure 2. Fold in on the crease to make a "V", figure 3.

figure 3

6 Repeat steps 2 through 5 with other wrappers.

7 Thread the two ends of one "V" shape through the two ends of the other, figure 4, creating a flat "V."

figure 4

8 Take another "V" and thread it through one of the ends so it begins a zigzag, figure 5.

figure 5

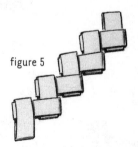

9 Keep repeating step 8 to create the chain.

20

Make Rubbings

Here's a great way for kids to explore and discover different textures, patterns, and shapes that exist in the environment around them. All you need are paper and crayons, pencils, or chalk; they can go out or stay in and find things to examine.

Simply put the paper over an object and rub the crayon on the paper. You will be left with an impression of the object. You can do rubbings of things such as coins, keys, pasta, string, jewelry, feathers, shells, rocks, and leaves, as well as various textured surfaces, including glass, wicker, bark, fabric, wood grain, and rugs.

SUPER TIP

Play hide & seek with your kids. You get to count to 50 or higher (and look at a magazine) while they hide. Take your time finding them—they love the suspense.

—DAWN, MOM OF TIMOTHY AND CARYS

Make a Kazoo

Many children make simple kazoos by folding a piece of waxed paper over the teeth of a comb and humming on the waxed paper. The vibration creates a kazoo-like sound. For even better sound, use a paper towel tube. Remind your kids that sound is a vibration so they can change their breath to alter the noise they make.

WHAT YOU'LL NEED
a paper towel tube
waxed paper
a rubber band

1 Cover one end of the tube with waxed paper. Use a rubber band to hold it flat and tight over the end.

2 Poke a hole in the tube above the end of the paper.

3 Hold the open end to your mouth and hum into it. You can try other types of paper or aluminum foil and see how the sound varies.

Make Blocks

Our baby-sitter had these big cardboard blocks and Richard loved to build with them, so I was often tempted to buy them, even though they are a lot of money for just five or 10 of them. It wasn't the expense that always made me hesitate; it was knowing I could make them myself—and, of course, knowing the kids could help.

Save tissue, cereal, rice, and other types of boxes, cover them with construction paper, and be done with it. When I get desperate over the amount of space they take up, I don't feel so bad recycling them.

SUPER TIP

Satisfy the "I wants" at the toy store with a simple, "Okay! Let's put it on the list for your birthday" then write it down, or let your child write it, on a list.

—KATHY, MOM OF JACK AND TOMMY

Crayon Scraping

This simple activity is a little messy and requires a pretty good attention span, but kid's are impressed by the results. You can actually buy black paper already prepared, but I always found that creating it was half the fun.

WHAT YOU'LL NEED
newspaper
plain white paper
different colors of crayons, including black
penny, key, or other hard-edged item

1 Lay newspaper on the work surface to contain the mess.

2 Completely color a piece of plain white paper with different crayons in any pattern.

3 Now, color over the whole thing with solid black crayon.

4 Using a penny, scrape away the black crayon to draw a picture by revealing the different colors underneath.

5 It's best to scrape in one direction to keep the color cleaner.

24

Play the Spoons

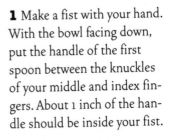

Anytime you take an ordinary everyday object and make it do something altogether different a child will think it's neat. To get the spoons to make noise you'll need to know a few basics. To really play them, though, you've got to have rhythm. Stainless-steel teaspoons are fine for beginners.

1 Make a fist with your hand. With the bowl facing down, put the handle of the first spoon between the knuckles of your middle and index fingers. About 1 inch of the handle should be inside your fist.

2 Put the other spoon over the knuckle of your index finger, with the bowl facing up. Hold it firmly with your thumb. Your thumb should extend parallel about 1 inch down the top of the spoon handle. The spoons should be aligned and the back of the bowls should be about ¼ inch apart from each other, figure 1.

figure 1

3 To play, tap the spoons to the beat between your thigh and your free hand. Each time you tap your thigh or hand, the back bowls of the spoons tap against one another.

4 You can sit, or stand and prop your leg up on a chair. The tip of the lower spoon comes down on the center of the thigh opposite the hand holding the spoons. After you tap the beat on your thigh, tap the offbeat with your free hand by holding it palm down and lightly meeting the top spoon with your fingertips.

5 To practice, first establish the beat on your thigh, and then add your offbeat. The accent you place on the beats establishes the rhythm. You can change your tempo by adjusting the speed at which you tap.

6 Add variety to your sound by bringing the bowl of the spoon down on different parts of your thigh or elsewhere on your body. For that matter, you can experiment on all different surfaces.

7 A nice move to show off is a finger drag. Open your fingers as wide as possible and with your palm facing you, drag the spoons over your fingers and follow that with a tap on your leg. Vary this by changing the number of fingers and the number of taps on the leg.

Make a Group Drawing

You may have seen toys that are cubes of wood divided into four layers. The top layer has a different head on each side, the next a different torso, the next different legs, and the bottom different feet. The idea is to turn each layer to create silly combinations. With just paper and a pencil, it's a fun way to pass time if you're waiting at a doctor's office.

1 Accordion fold a piece of paper into quarters.

2 One person draws a head on the top section. Then she folds the paper so her drawing is hidden and the second section is face up. She should extend the lines of the neck slightly onto the second section to indicate where the next person should draw.

3 The next person draws the torso on the second section, using the lines the previous person drew as a guide. Then he marks on the third section where the legs should begin and folds the paper so the third section is face up and the first two are hidden.

4 The next person draws the legs and indicates the end of the legs with short lines at the top of the last section. She also folds the paper so the drawings are hidden.

5 The last person draws the feet on the bottom section where the lines indicate.

6 Unfold the paper to see what the creature looks like.

26

Make a Tambourine

There are a variety of easy ways to make a tambourine—or if you want a band—a bunch of tambourines that each make a different noise. My favorite is to put some beans, beads, or rice (in a pinch, NERDS or another hard, small candy will work) between two aluminum pie tins and tape the tins together.

You can do the same with a couple of paper plates stapled or glued together. Yet another way is to attach some jingle bells with ribbon or yarn to a plastic plate. If you use paper plates, your child can color them. An aluminum pie tin tambourine can be decorated by gluing on streamers, yarn, or construction paper.

SUPER TIP

When the kids are getting really loud and you need some peace play a few rounds of who can be quiet the longest.

—NICK, DAD OF RICHARD, ANITA AND JOHN

Play Princess and the Pea

We played this at my daughter's third birthday party. The theme was princesses, so we played pin the tiara on Cinderella (even though my son pointed out that she doesn't wear a tiara), musical "thrones," and Princess and the Pea. The last was the most fun for everyone. They all wanted another turn. I read The Princess and the Pea before we played to help them understand the game. To this day, my daughter still asks me for "a pea" so she can play.

WHAT YOU'LL NEED

three pillows
small ball or marble (depending on the thickness of the pillows and the sensitivity and age of the children)

1 Place the three pillows in a row on the floor.

2 Have the child close her eyes while you place the "pea" under one of the pillows.

3 Have the child sit on each pillow, one at a time, and guess which pillow the pea is under.

28

Make a Bowling Set

Kids love to knock things down, so bowling is a great sport for them—it focuses their throwing energy into something positive (which comes in handy when you're inside). There are many different sets you could buy for your home, or you could easily make your own.

WHAT YOU'LL NEED

10 1 liter plastic bottles or plastic baby bottles
colored tape

Remove the labels from the bottles. Wash them and allow them to dry thoroughly. Decorate the bottles with stripes using the tape. Grab a ball. Set up the "pins" and bowl.

SUPER TIP

Use coasters to play memory games because often a set of eight will have four sets of matching patterns.

—ANNA, MOM OF MATTHEW AND ADRIEL

Play Paper Football

Historically, this game seems to have been played covertly in classrooms around the country. Although that may not be the smartest application, it is a good way to pass time when you are stuck waiting with not much more than a friend, a table, and a sheet of paper.

1 First you need to make your football.

* Fold a piece of 8.5 x 11-inch paper lengthwise into thirds, figure 1. Then fold the top edge over to align with the side edge, forming a triangle at the top.

* Fold that triangle down, figure 2. Then fold the top edge to the other side edge. Continue folding the triangle down until you have just a short end.

* Fold the end into a pointed tab and tuck it into the pocket on the triangle, figure 3.

2 Two players sit across the table from one another. The first player lays the football flat on the table in front of him and flicks it with his finger across the table. (Depending on the age of your child, she can get one or three flicks in an effort to get a touchdown.) If the football stops with part of it hanging over the edge of the table, it's a touchdown, which is worth six points. If it falls off the table, it's the other player's turn.

3 After a touchdown, the player may kick a field goal. The opponent forms the goalpost. He holds his hands in fists, palms facing out, thumb outstretched to touch his opposing thumb, and his forefingers pointing up. Or for a wider goal, he turns his hands so the palms are facing in, with his forefingers touching and his thumbs pointing up. He holds the goalpost at his edge of the table. The kicker stands the ball up on the table with her finger, the long edge facing her and the point facing her opponent. The kicker flicks the ball; if it goes between the posts she scores one point.

figure 1

4 The game can be a predetermined number of turns and the player with the highest score wins, or a predetermined score and the first one to reach it wins. Or they can simply play until they are both bored.

figure 2

figure 3

Play Penny Basketball

This is a great game for vacations. Or play it in a restaurant while you're waiting for the food to come. It's only for older kids, though, because the pennies are a choking hazard.

1 The players sit opposite one another at a table.

2 One player makes a "V" with his forefinger and middle finger and holds it flat on the table (knuckles up), centered in front of him.

3 The other player arranges the pennies flat on the table in a triangle in front of her, the base of the triangle closest to her. She slides them across the table by flicking them with her finger. (The table surface needs to be smooth for the pennies to slide well.)

4 She then tries to get one of the pennies into her opponent's "V." However, she must flick one penny at a time and it must pass between the other two pennies. She does this until she either gets a point, by getting the penny into the "V," or knocks a penny off the table. The players take turns until one player has reached the agreed-upon winning score.

31

Make Ring Toss

This is another game that you could buy, but why bother when you can easily make it with paper towel tubes and cardboard? This game can be used for small children (to practice their throwing and aim) or older kids (they can keep score and stand further away from the stakes).

WHAT YOU'LL NEED
2 paper towel tubes
2 paper plates
cardboard
paint
glue

1 Paint two paper towel tubes with two different colors. Glue each one standing on end to the center of a paper plate. These are the stakes.

2 Cut six 8-inch circles out of cardboard. Cut out the center of each one, leaving a 2-inch brim. Paint three to match one stake and three to match the other stake.

Play Jacks

Truth be told, I was never very good at playing jacks. But I had them, and when there was no one around to play with, I practiced alone. It's a game intended for two or more players, but kids find it challenging and fun to play alone just to see how far they can get.

WHAT YOU'LL NEED

a set of jacks—a small bouncy ball and five to fifteen jacks (whatever comes in the set)

a good surface for bouncing the ball (a hard floor is better than a table).

1 Throw the jacks onto the floor, then toss the ball in the air, pick up one jack, and catch the ball in the same hand before the ball bounces a second time (or at all, if you want to make it more difficult). You can put the caught jacks in the other hand.

2 Continue doing this until you've picked up all the jacks. When you've completed "onesies," continue with "twosies." You play this the same as onesies, but you pick up two jacks at a time. Keep going until you pick up all jacks on one toss, or until you miss and the next player tries. The player that picks up the most jacks at one time is the winner.

33

GAME

Give Slug Rides

Richard introduced this to the family. I think he made it up on his own, which makes it even more special. I love it because it's original and simple. Plus, all the kids can play togther, no one gets hurt, there's no fighting and they all have fun.

He lies on his stomach on the floor and John or Anita sits on his back. He slides along like a snail on his belly. They love it, and it's not too rough for them.

SUPER TIP

Put numbers or colors on the back of puzzle pieces so you can tell which is which if they get mixed up.

—HARRIET, MOM OF TOMMY, KATHY, DAVID, DANNY, BRIAN,

CAROLYN, SUSAN AND JANE

Play Rock, Paper, Scissors

When Richard began with the "I'm first" and the "No, my way," my husband taught him rock, paper, scissors. Richard and Anita enjoy it so much that it isn't just played for deciding arguments—it's played purely for the fun of the game. The game is best played with two people, but more than two can also play.

1 Someone (or everyone, in unison) says, "Rock, paper, scissors, shoot."

2 Both players simultaneously put out a rock (a fist), paper (a flat hand, palm down), or scissors (a "V" made with the forefinger and the middle finger).

3 The hierarchy of the objects determines the winner. Scissors cut paper, paper covers rock, rock smashes scissors.

4 With three or more players you have to keep shooting until one of the three options is not displayed. You also have to have elimination rounds. For example, if there are five players and three rocks and two papers are thrown out, the rocks are out and the papers face off.

GAME | 🚫

Make a Fortune Teller

t's funny how certain things you did when you were a child can get buried so deeply in the recesses of your mind yet arise instantaneously when your five-year-old comes home and says, "Look, Mom! Look what we made at school today!!!"

WHAT YOU'LL NEED
sheet of paper
scissors
crayons or markers

1 You need a square sheet of paper. If you are starting with a rectangle, fold it over so the short edge aligns with the long edge. This makes a double triangle with an extra single edge. Cut the excess piece from the bottom.

2 Open the triangle and fold it again so the other corners meet. Open it again so you have a square with crisscrossing creases.

3 Now fold each corner care-

figure 1

figure 2

figure 3

figure 4

fully so the points meet in the center where the creases cross, figures 1 & 2.

4 Turn the paper over so the flat side is face up. Again fold the corners carefully so they meet in the center.

5 Turn the paper over so the squares face up. With crayons, color each square a color, and write the color on the square, figure 3.

6 Turn over the paper so the triangles face up and write a number on one side of each triangle. Open each triangle and write a fortune behind each number. Try messages such as: "Today is your lucky day," "You'll have fun tomorrow," and "You have good friends." figure 4.

7 Fold the triangles back over and fold the resulting

square in half along the horizontal and vertical centers to form creases.

8 With the square folded in half, insert your thumbs and forefingers into each colored pocket, front and back, and bring the outside corners together in the center, forming a sort of pyramid shape, figure 5. You're ready to play.

9 Ask someone to choose a color. Spell the color out loud, closing and opening the fortune-teller for each letter.

10 When you're done, have the person pick one of the numbers from those visible. Open and close the fortune-teller that amount of times. Repeat this step.

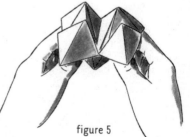

figure 5

11 Have the person pick another number then read the fortune behind that number.

Make & Play Activity Dice

Apparently, preschools across the country use variations of this game to keep kids active on days when they can't go outside. You can make up the activities you want to put onto the dice, the more physical, the better.

WHAT YOU'LL NEED

two empty small square tissue boxes
construction paper
markers or crayons

1 First, make the dice with two tissue boxes by gluing colored construction paper onto each side.

2 Then on one cube, number each side one through six.

3 On the other cube, write activities such as jump on both feet, hop on one foot, spin, touch your toes, pat your head, and clap your hands.

4 The kids take turns rolling the dice and doing the activity the number of times indicated.

37

Play Rafts with Rugs

This is a game that my sister-in-law plays with her daughter, Elena. This is a good example of being a superhero—I look at the floor and the rugs everyday, but I never thought of turning them into a game. The area rugs are rafts and the floor is the water.

Sometimes the water is shallow and they wade in it and splash around. Sometimes they swim from one raft to another, where they can sit and play games such as patty-cake. Occasionally, Elena may venture out to save a stuffed toy and bring it aboard.

SUPER TIP

Have your kids make birthday cards for friends and relatives. It will teach them about giving and the recipients will enjoy the gift.

—JENNIFER, MOM OF MAX AND SAM

Thumb Wrestle

This is a classic game, perfect for playing while waiting for dinner to be served at a restaurant on while on line at Disney World. Even really little kids can do this—of course, you'll have to let them win or else they won't want to keep playing.

1 Each player uses her right hand. The two players grip each other's four fingers leaving the thumbs free to fight. Their thumbs face each other at the top.

2 In unison, the players say, "One, two, three, four, I declare a thumb war." At each count of the rhyme, they touch their thumbs down on opposite sides, alternating sides on each line of the rhyme.

3 Once they've finished the introduction, the players attempt to pin the other person's thumb down with her thumb.

4 You can't lift your elbow or wrist to gain an advantage, nor can you use your other hand.

Have Wheelbarrow Races

Because I came from a large family, we didn't need to have a party in order to have races. With a smaller family you'll need to invite some friends for a race. In the meantime, you and your child can practice together, make sure you don't walk too fast for her—it takes a good bit of strength to hold yourself up.

1 One child lies on the floor and puts her palms flat on the floor beside her chest.

2 The other person holds her ankles or shins around his waist.

3 As he lifts her legs up, the "wheelbarrow" pushes her weight up onto her hands.

4 They both begin to walk, she on her hands and he on his feet.

SUPER TIP

Put your children in front of a full-length mirror and have them pretend to whine, cry, laugh, etc. I've caught my son entertaining himself this way on more than one occasion .

—PEGGY, MOM OF SEAN

Get Your Toddler to Brush

I don't remember who suggested this to me, but I have relied on it morning and night for my toddlers. It has proven effective for neighbors and friends as well. Of course, you could just buy an electric toothbrush that looks like a superhero. That's what my friend Donna did.

Just pick your child's latest fascination—Barbie, Elmo, Ranger, the dog next door—and look for the character in his mouth. Lately for John my 2-year-old, it's Ranger. The game goes like this:

ME: "Okay, John, let's brush those teeth."

JOHN: "NO!"

ME: "Oh! Who's that in your mouth? Is that Ranger?"

✳ He opens his mouth and I get started. If he starts to close I say, "Uh oh, there he goes, he's over here now. Oh, he's barking. Ruff ruff!" I continue the monologue until the job is done.

✳ It works every time, though sometimes I need to try several characters before I get the one that works. Anita, my 4-year-old, even tells me whom to look for.

41

Fix Plastic Toys

This doesn't require the greatest of skills or talent, but it will make you a hero in the eyes of your children. Kids are usually distraught when their toys break and they get even more upset when you try to glue the broken toy together but your solution fails.

The key is to get the right kind of glue. It's not Elmer's, and it's not Superglue. Instead, go the hardware store and look for "Testors Plastic Cement" (or go online to www.hobbylinc.com). Tell your child that the toy needs time to dry.

SUPER TIP

A great way to get the giggles out is to tell your child that NO MATTER WHAT they are not allowed to laugh. Then tickle them.

—MARY, MOM OF JAMES AND ALEX

42

Cover a Book

My mom probably covered hundreds of textbooks in her lifetime—which is probably why she had a technique for making a cover that stayed secure for the entire school year. She used brown paper grocery bags, but you can use any heavy paper and let your kids decorate them.

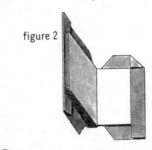

figure 1

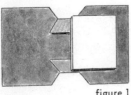

figure 2

figure 3

WHAT YOU'LL NEED
brown grocery bag or other heavy paper
scissors
pencil
tape

1 Lay the book open on the paper. Cut the paper so it is about 2 ½ inches bigger than the book on all sides.

2 Center the book's spine on the paper from both side to side and top to bottom.

3 Draw a line on the paper along the top and bottom edges of the spine, about 1 inch past the spine's edge.

4 From the ends of these lines draw lines about 45 degrees diagonally out to the edge of the paper.

5 Cut along the four diagonal lines from the paper edge to the horizontal line, creating two tabs. Fold the tabs onto the center of the paper.

6 Place the book on the paper so the spine is centered. The spine should align with the folded edges, figure 1.

7 With the book closed, tightly fold the ends of the paper around the front and back covers.

8 With the spine perpendicular to you and one cover

flat on the table, hold the other cover and the pages up in your hand.

9 Starting with the far corner, create a 45-degree edge from the corner of the book to the top edge of the paper by tucking the top layer of the fold behind the book cover, figure 2.

10 Fold the resulting flap onto the inside cover and tape it along the fold in the corner, figure 3.

11 Turn the book and repeat steps 8 through 10 on the remaining three corners.

Teach a Child to Tie Shoes

You are probably familiar with some type of rhyme that is intended to help teach your child to tie his or her shoes. I knew the one about the rabbit ears but never found it that helpful. That is, until my sister in-law, Lynn, showed me this technique:

1 Use a belt from an adult bathrobe.

2 Sit your child on your lap facing forward.

3 Demonstrate the mechanics of tying a shoelace with the belt around his waist.

4 Once your child is able to tie the belt around his waist, he can try tying his shoelaces.

5 If bending down to the shoes on his feet is still too challenging, him first get the hang of it with the shoes on his lap.

6 In case you don't know the rhyme, here's one I like best .
* Build a tepee
(cross the two ends)
* Come inside (bring one lace around the other)
* Close it tight so we can hide (pull the knot)
* Over the mountain (make a loop)
* And around we go (bring the other lace around)
* Here's my arrow (bring the lace through the hole forming the second loop)
* And here's my bow! (pull tight)

44

Teach your Kids to Dance

Dancing with the kids gets some energy out on days (or at night) when you can't go outside. Although it's true that kids will just dance without needing to know how, it is my belief that every four-year-old is happy to learn the Shimmy, the Twist, the Swim, and the Pony, not to mention the Hokey Pokey. But you should also feel free to teach them any version of the Hustle or even swing dancing.

Pick out songs that are about dancing, such as "The Locomotion" (Little Eva) and "Land of 1,000 Dances" (Wilson Pickett) to teach the Pony and the Swim; "The Hustle" (Van McCoy) to teach partner dancing; "The Twist" (Chubby Checker) to let them dance alone; and "Jump, Jive, and Wail" (Brian Setzer) to teach swing dancing.

SUPER TIP

Have one of the older kids teach one of the younger kids a new game or a new skill. They'll both feel special.

—MADONNA, MOM OF ELISABETH AND THOMAS

45

Tie a Necktie

Clip-on ties are fine for a couple of years, but don't be caught unprepared the day your son needs to wear a real tie. The four-in-hand knot is very simple, and your son could do it himself once you show him how. The Windsor knot, on the other hand, is a complicated but more impressive knot. Here are the instructions for both:

figure 1

figure 2

figure 3

THE FOUR-IN-HAND KNOT

1 Hang the tie around your neck, seam side down. The wide side of the tie should be on the side of your dominant hand. The narrow end should be just above the fourth button on the shirt.

2 Bring the broad end across the front of the narrow end, then behind, figure 1, and across the front again.

3 Next, bring the broad end up and through the space between your neck and the tie, figure 2, and let the broad end hang down in front.

4 Now thread the broad end through the loop at the front, figure 3.

5 Use two hands to tighten and straighten the knot.

6 According to my husband, it's looks best if the front of the tie has a dimple just at the base of the knot. You create the dimple by poking the front with your index finger and pinching the two sides when you tighten and straighten.

THE WINDSOR

1 Hang the tie around your neck, seam side down. The wide side should be on the side of your dominant hand. The narrow end should be just above the fourth button on the shirt.

figure 4

figure 5

figure 6

figure 7

figure 8

2 Bring the broad end across the front of the narrow end and up through the space between your neck and the tie, figure 4.

3 Wrap the broad end around the back and bring it to the left side, then over the top and through the space. Pull it back out to the left. The seam will be facing out, figure 5.

4 Bring the broad end across the front of the knot to the right side, figure 6, then bring it up through the back of the space, figure 7.

5 Thread it down through the loop in the front, figure 8.

6 Tighten and straighten the knot carefully with two hands.

SKILL

Draw Cartoon Characters

Knowing how to draw simple, funny drawings is a great skill when you have kids because it's a good way to entertain them in restaurants, especially restaurants with paper tablecloths, and crayons already on the table. Plus, you can show your kids how to do it themselves.

* Start with a basic shape—a circle, square, rectangle, or triangle-for a head. Add to that other basic shapes for bodies and extremities. (In other words, don't try to draw perfect arms and legs; instead, aim for shapes you can actually accomplish if you're not an artist.)

* To add personality and features (eyes, ears, nose, etc.), add more shapes or lines without worrying, once again, about making them look perfect. Funny is good. Big teeth and big ears are always funny.

* Add curved lines around the character to show action and add scenery (sun, moon, houses, trees, flowers) to tell a story.

Tell Right Shoe from Left

My neighbor Carolyn gave me a cute and simple tip to help Anita learn which shoe goes on which foot. This is one of those things that toddlers want so much to learn, but it's actually harder for them to learn than you would think.

With a pen Carolyn drew eyes and a smile on the instep of each shoe. Then she told Anita that when she puts her shoes on, the faces should always be smiling at each other. It worked for us.

If you don't want to draw on your child's shoes, you can draw on a piece of tape or use smiley stickers.

SUPER TIP

*Post family "rules" that the children have helped write.
They'll be more inclined to follow rules they've helped compose.
Also, recalling which rule they're breaking will distract
them from continuing the offensive action.*

—BETH, MOM OF JACK

48

Make Up a Story (starring your kids)

You may not be Danielle Steel or Stephen King, but here is the basis of any story: Boy meets girl, boy gets girl, boy loses girl, boy gets girl again. Or, in the case of boys who aren't yet ready to chase girls, the point is: The hero finds herself up against a challenge, the hero almost wins the challenge, the hero almost loses the challenge, and the hero tries again and finally wins. Who is the hero? Well, your favorite five-year-old, of course.

1 Using your knowledge of your hero-child, figure out what her challenge will be—fighting dragons, hitting a home run, or going to the dentist.

2 You can use a pseudonym if you'd like, but many of the children I know actually want to star in these stories, even if the point of the story is unbelievably obvious.

3 Use a lot of hyperbolic adjectives to describe the hero, as well as the other characters in the story—"the beautiful, lovely, and generous Lady Marissa," for example. (It always helps to make the heroes princes and princesses or lords and ladies. Everyone loves to be royalty; don't worry about making the titles match the royal lineage.)

4 Set the scene in an outdoor place, but don't make it the final destination. For example, if the goal is for Lady Marissa to get to the dentist, have her start out in the forest (symbolizing her fear).

5 Set the mood regarding the challenge—remember to put in the challenge and the potential prize. "Lady Marissa found herself in the forest and a dragon came up to her and said, 'In order to get the priceless diamond, you must go to the dentist and let him clean your teeth!'"

6 Remember that this is a challenge, so Lady Marissa has to know what her fears would be. This is good, because it will reassure the young lady that her fears are normal. "Lady Marissa was frightened because she had heard that dentists could hurt princesses with their sharp tools."

7 Introduce someone or something that will help the princess-her favorite toy; her mommy; or even a surprising friend, such as her baby brother, Lord Caleb the Drooler (a laugh is never a bad thing). "Suddenly, Lord Caleb the Drooler came upon the scene and said to the dragon, 'Lady Marissa doesn't have to go the dentist because her teeth can rot! She's a princess no matter what!'"

8 At this point, Lady Marissa is going to have to face her challenge. Will she go to the dentist or will she let her teeth rot? Remember that she is eventually going to have to fight for going to the dentist. In other words, this isn't the scene of the big battle—it's the scene that sets the stage for the big battle. So, begin by allowing Lady Marissa to mull through her options. (At this point, it's most likely that Lady Marissa will have a few thoughts of her own to contribute.)

9 Now, this is important. Have Lady Marissa decide to stay far away from the dentist or, even better, make her decide to go, but have it be difficult for her to get there. The dragon, for example, could breathe fire and knock down a tree to block her way. Or suddenly a witch could appear and try to eat her up (make sure the witch has rotted teeth—this witch won't LET little children go to the dentist because she knows it's good for them).

10 Now it's time for Lady Marissa and Lord Caleb the Drooler to fight their way to the dentist. They are brave and they are heroes, after all. Make sure the battle is dramatic and, quite possibly, almost bloody.

You don't think I'm going to tell you the end, do you? That's for you to make up.

Get Your Toddler to Dress

I started this technique with Anita, and then John when they were babies. John and I play every day while I dress him so he expects to laugh and have some fun and he doesn't resist putting on his clothes. Now four, Anita still sometimes asks me to do it with her.

When I put John's shirt on, before his head comes through the collar, I say, "Where's Johnny?" I pull down the shirt and when his face pops through I act very surprised and say, "There he is!" He laughs every time. Then I do it with his arms. "Now, where are Johnny's hands?" When he pushes one through I say, "Oh, There it is!" and so on to the feet.

SUPER TIP

Sing and dance with your kids, and not just to their music; turn them on to your favorites. It helps you bond, gives you an aura of coolness, and it's just plain old-fashioned fun!

—DEB, MOM OF DANNY AND REBECCA

50

Perform Magic Tricks

*I*t's always good to know one or
two magic tricks, especially
some that don't involve any special materials and that are simple
enough for your kids to do once
you let them in on the secret. They
will have fun doing the trick and
will also enjoy that you shared the
secret with them.

VANISHING COIN TRICK

*You need only a coin, a table, a
chair, and good sleight of hand.*
1 Show your audience that
you have an ordinary coin. Tell
them you will make it disap-
pear by rubbing it on your
elbow. Rub it on your elbow
and recite a magic incantation.

2 After a while stop and put
the coin on the table. Tell
your audience that it sometimes works better on the
other elbow.

figure 1

3 Pick up the coin and pretend to put it in the other hand and pretend to rub it on the other elbow. In fact, while it is still in the first hand, drop it down the back collar of your shirt, figure 1.

4 Show the audience that it has disappeared and that both hands are empty.

HOPPING RUBBER BAND

This gives the impression that a rubber band hops from one set of fingers to another. All you need are two rubber bands.

1 Show the audience your rubber bands. Place one over your index and middle fingers; allow it to rest at the base, figure 2.

2 Hold up your hand so the back is toward the audience. With your other hand, pull

figure 2

the rubber band out toward you, demonstrating that it is intact.

3 While it is pulled out, bend your fingers down so the all the tips are inside the loop, figure 3.

figure 3

4 Straighten your fingers, and the rubber band will jump to your ring and pinky fingers, figure 4.

5 You can make it jump back by repeating steps 2 through 4.

figure 4

6 Next, keep the rubber band around your ring and index fingers and twist the second rubber band once around the top of each finger, so they are looped together, figure 5.

7 Do the trick again and one rubber band seems to pass through the other.

figure 5

51

Make Up a Song (starring your kids)

I realized I was a closet Paul McCartney when I wanted to teach my oldest son our address. Knowing that if you put information to music you won't forget it, I decided to find a way to sing our address. I picked a melody that had already been composed, and voilà! At age two, Richard could sing where we lived, as well as his full name and how to spell his first name.

1 Pick a melody you-and everyone else-can't get out of your head, such as:

"B-I-N-G-O"

"Old MacDonald"

"Happy Birthday"

"John Brown's Baby"

"Jingle Bells"

"Row, Row, Row Your Boat"

"Twinkle, Twinkle Little Star"

"On Top of Old Smoky"

2 Don't pick a song with three verses, a chorus, and a bridge! Just pick a short and simple melody. Or pick the chorus of a song—that's usually the catchiest part. Also, advertising jingles are always catchy and they work well with short messages, such as names, addresses, phone numbers, and other important information that your kids should remember.

3 Figure out what you want to sing about—your daughter's favorite doll, your son's birthday. Whatever it is, pick one topic because you'll only compose four or five lines at the most.

4 Start to sing, repeating the melody and playing with the words. Don't fear repetition. Where would Sir Paul be if he couldn't sing the words "Love Me Do" over and over? (Actually, now that I think about it, that's not a bad chorus to keep in mind for your compositions.) Let your kids sing with you. You don't have to teach them a perfect song. Eventually, you'll all come up with a finished version. Here's one a friend of mine did:

(To the tune of "John Brown's Baby")
I live on Sandpiper Lane
I live on Sandpiper Lane
I live on Sandpiper Lane
In Rockport, Massachusetts
And another:
(to the tune of "J-E-L-L-O")
J-A-M-E-S

Change your Toddler

Some kids lie quietly when its times for their diapers to be changed, while others can't stand stopping their playtime for something so practical and boring. For those times when your toddler is too busy to stop and have his diaper changed my sister-in-law Linda has this suggestion:

On the changing table pretend the little fussbudget is Lance Armstrong. Pump his legs up and down say, "Connor's riding the bike. He's riding up the hill slower and slower. Oh, so steep. He's at the top. He's going down. He's going faster and faster." As your voice gets higher and faster and his legs go faster and faster before you know it he is cracking up and can't remember why he didn't want to be there.

SUPER TIP

Don't put kids' socks and shoes on until just before you leave the house, unless you want to do it twice.

—SUSAN, MOM OF RICHARD, ANITA AND JOHN

How to Juggle

I learned to juggle when I was single and working at a job that required a significant amount of waiting time. It's a talent that has served me well as a parent. My oldest son is especially impressed that I know how to juggle, though he himself has not wanted to learn. He frequently asks me to demonstrate my ability, and I'm always happy to show off my trick.

1 First you need a set of three balls that fit nicely in your hands. Slightly squishy balls that don't bounce and won't roll away easily when dropped are good for beginners. Beanbags also work well. Stand in front of a bed or couch so that you don't move forward as you toss the balls. Also, when you drop the balls you won't have to bend too far to pick them up.

2 Start with one ball. Keep your hands at about waist level and toss the ball in an arc at about eye level. Allow the ball to come back down to waist

figure 1

level and catch it in the other hand. Keep tossing one ball back and forth in this manner until it feels comfortable.

3 Once you are comfortable with one ball, add a second ball. Hold one ball in each hand. Throw the first ball as you learned in step 2. As that ball is at the top of its arc, throw the second ball in an arc. (The upward path of the second ball should cross the upward path of the first ball, figure 1.) Catch the first ball. Catch the second ball. Repeat this, but begin with the opposite hand. Continue back and forth until it feels comfortable. Take your time getting comfortable with two balls before adding the third.

4 Hold two balls in one hand (in your right hand if you're a

figure 2

righty, in your left if you're a lefty) and one in the other. Toss the front of the two balls from the two-fisted hand into the air in an arc, figure 2. Toss the ball in the opposite hand in an opposing arc, figure 3 (as you did with the two-ball toss in step 3). Catch the first ball. Before catching the second ball, toss the third ball in an arc to the opposite hand, figure 4. Before catching the third ball, toss the first ball. All three balls are now in constant motion. Remember, once you have tossed the first ball you will not have two balls in your hands at the same time again. Continue to toss before you catch; toss, catch, toss, catch from hand to hand. One ball is always in the air, and only one ball is in each hand at any one time.

figure 3

figure 4

54

Organize the Toys

I f you live in a house, there are probably bikes, scooters, and a variety of other vehicles and toys cluttering up your garage or scattered around your yard. Here is a way to straighten up while, at the same time, reinforce your childrens' reading skills.

1 Label your storage areas. Multi-colored chalk shows up well on both unfinished garage beams and unpainted walls. Write words such as chalk, balls, bikes, bats, scooters, etc.

2 If your children can't yet read, draw pictures of the items. This helps the kids learn words, since they associate the words with the picture.

3 You can do the same thing inside with labels on plastic bins or baskets that hold cars, legos, dolls, books, etc. Then store them on shelves.

SUPER TIP

Exercise with with your children. Mine likes to get on the floor and do yoga with me. But even taking a walk around the block is fun for them and good for both of you.

—DONNA, MOM OF JAMES

Take a Child's Photograph

I used to be the art director of Parenting *magazine, so I attended lots of photo shoots with children and, in the process, learned a few tricks about how to get kids to look at the camera and maybe even smile. We had the benefit of having a very wonderful baby wrangler, which of course you don't have at home, but that doesn't mean you can't employ some of her trade secrets. You'll need another person to help you (this is a situation where less is usually more)—one person (usually the parent) does the wrangling and one does the photographing.*

1 The wrangler should stand with their head close to the camera so the child looks at the camera.

2 One trick to get the child to stay in place is to put tape or stickers on the floor and have her try to unstick them.

3 When you want the child to look at the camera, tell him to look for Elmo/Dora/the kitty in the lens. That will get him for a short while.

4 Pretend sneezes will sometimes make kids laugh a lot.

5 Singing "Happy Birthday" to the child is usually better than singing any other song.

6 Wear something silly on your head or, if you can, tape something silly on the top of your lens.

7 For candid photographs have a camera (even a disposable one) in your diaper bag and take a picture when they least expect it rather than having the child pose.

56

Observe Worms

've seen other methods for building worm homes, but Richard and I like this one best. You and your children will be able to observe the activity of the worms more clearly because of the internal core of this home. Remember, any mom who picks up worms is a superhero to her kids!

WHAT YOU'LL NEED

scissors
2-liter clear plastic bottle
1-liter clear plastic bottle
gravel
small amount of coffee
grounds (optional; worms
like coffee grounds)
dark, moist soil
sand
dead leaves (worms prefer
maple to oak)
grass cuttings
some earthworms
black plastic bag that doesn't
allow light in

1 With scissors, cut the top off the 2-liter bottle, then wash both bottles.

2 Fill the 1-liter bottle with water and place it in the center of the 2-liter bottle. The water helps keep the worms cool.

3 Put a layer of gravel around the smaller bottle.

4 Mix the coffee grounds, if using, with the soil.

5 On top of the gravel, put in a ¾-inch layer of soil, then a ¾-inch layer of sand. Alternate soil and sand until the space between the two bottles is almost full.

6 Fill the remaining space with a mixture of leaves and grass cuttings.

7 Place the worms on top of the mixture.

8 Cover the worm home with the black plastic bag.

9 Place it in a cool dark spot where it won't be disturbed.

10 Check in on your worms after a few hours, days, a week, and then two weeks. Observe how they moved within the home.

11 Keep the soil moist by watering it with a spray bottle if it begins to dry out. But don't make it muddy because the worms could drown if it's too wet.

12 Finally, return the worms to the spot where you found them.

SUPER TIP

Keep a dictionary of words your child has asked about; after you look up the new word, write it in their "dictionary."

—SUSAN, MOM OF RICHARD, ANITA AND JOHN

Use a Remote Control Car

There are two ways to play with radio-controlled cars. The first is simply to let your kids race them around the driveway and street. Which one goes the fastest? You can use traffic cones (available at most hardware stores) to set up a racing area.

The second way is to draw a racetrack on the street or in the driveway with chalk. Make sure it has plenty of straightaways, because it's often difficult for kids to steer well. Also, make lanes so that more than one kid can race at the same time. You can make a big figure eight, but those are actually tough to maneuver, especially for kids. If your kid has trouble driving the car, have her first drive straight ahead and backward and not worry about turning.

SUPER TIP
---

*Let your child help clean out one of your closets
(she'll love trying on your clothes, shoes and purses).*

—ALICE, MOM OF LAURA AND SAMANTHA

58

Make a Fairy House

When you're outside doing yard work and your children are looking for something to do, building a fairy house is a perfect activity. A fairy house is a small dwelling built in a somewhat hidden spot.
The theory is that once built it provides a resting spot for fairies.

WHAT YOU'LL NEED
Twigs, stones, leaves, grass
cuttings, maple seedlings,
dandelion seeds, moss,
feathers, dried-up flowers,
pinecones, acorns, shells,
and bark all work great.

1 Gather the supplies. This is
the part that will keep the kids
out of your hair for a while, so
make sure they collect lots of
building materials!

2 Next, pick a spot to build
the fairy house. According to
lore, it should be in a somewhat sheltered spot, not out
in the open. But you'll want to
pick a spot that allows enough
room for your child to work,
and for you to help, without
trampling your garden.

3 It's a good idea to build it
against a tree or at the base of
a bush or shrub for support.
Or you can jam the main support twigs into the ground and
support them with pebbles.

4 Once the house is sturdy,
you can leave your child to
finish the building; create
walks, gardens, and fences;
and do the decorating. He or
she may want to make a bed,
some chairs, and a table.

Make a Whistle with Grass

Like wishes made on dandelion seeds and helicopters created from maple seeds, you need to share this activity with a child—any child—for her sake and yours. It's one of the pure, simple joys in life. Don't forget to lie on the grass and look at the sky while you do this.

1 First you need to find a long blade of grass. Crabgrass is perfect: wide and stiff.

2 Hold one end flat between the top of your thumb (along the edge of your nail) and your forefinger.

3 Hold the grass in place and slide the other thumb joint

downward against the first.

4 Press the outer edges of your thumbs together, joint to joint, knuckle to knuckle, with the nails facing you.

5 When the grass is firmly in position, release your forefinger. The blade of grass is held taut across the gap formed between your knuckles and your joints, figure 1.

6 Bring your thumbs to your lips and blow on the gap. The sound is loud and a bit squeaky, like air being let out of a balloon. You may end up sorry you demonstrated this simple pleasure after all.

figure 1

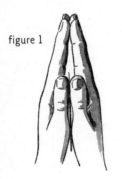

Make Bubble Juice

O ne of the doctors at my pediatrician's office has a small bottle of bubbles that she wears around her neck in case she has any reluctant patients. At home, you can keep bubbles at the changing table for a distraction. When your kids get older and you really start going through the bubble juice, you can make your own with dishwashing liquid and water.

1 Mix together 1 cup of water and 2 tablespoons of dishwashing liquid.

2 If you don't have a bubble wand, you can blow bubbles with a drinking straw.

SUPER TIP

For kids' birthdays let them choose whatever they want for breakfast and make it and then serve it to them in bed. It's a great way to make them feel extra special.

—VIVIAN, MOM OF KYLE AND NICOLE

Make Fossils

Two types of commonly found fossils are impressions of things left in hardened dirt or three-dimensional casts of things created when an impression was filled with sediment. The first fossil I made was a scallop shell. It made such an impression on me; I can still remember admiring it.

WHAT YOU'LL NEED

scissors
empty cardboard milk carton
object, such as a shell
petroleum jelly
container and spoon for mixing the plaster
plaster of Paris

1 With scissors, cut off the top of the milk carton so the bottom piece is about 3 inches deep.

2 Coat the object with petroleum jelly.

3 Using a container and spoon, mix a batch of plaster of Paris according to the package directions and pour it into the carton.

4 When it begins to set, press the object into the plaster and carefully remove it, leaving behind an impression.

5 Allow the mold to harden completely.

6 Coat the impression with petroleum jelly.

7 Make a new batch of plaster. Pour it onto the impression.

8 When it has hardened, separate the top from the bottom. This is the cast.

Make Sand Toys

The pool club my family and I go to has a sandbox, which is really more of a sand yard. It's a big area where big kids and little kids have plenty of room to play. The big ones are usually working together on complicated structures involving rivers, tunnels, mountains, and pools. It has nothing to do with sandcastles; it's all about water and digging. Scattered around the sand are an assortment of pails and shovels of all shapes and sizes. The most coveted, however, are the big scoops some ingenious parent made from large laundry detergent bottles.

When the detergent bottle (the bigger the better) is empty, wash it out well and then cut off the bottom. Keep the cap on, and the scoop serves a dual purpose: a shovel for the sand and a vessel for carrying water. The caps by themselves, once cleaned, are good for younger kids to use as cups in the sand or water.

SUPER TIP

Save the big cardboard box from a television or other large appliance for hours of fun. It could be so many things: a cave, a fort, a car, a castle, or simply a box that the kids hide in and play with, as is.

—CAROLYN, MOM OF HUGO AND CELESTE

63

A Good Paper Airplane

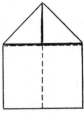

figure 1

figure 2

figure 3

My idea of the best paper airplane may not be the same as anyone else's. In fact, my friend Donna told me that three of her former boyfriends claimed to know how to make the best paper airplane. Each one was different. While I was doing research to determine my choice model, two dads demonstrated their favorite models (again, each was different). For me, the best plane needs to meet the following criteria:

* It needs to fly well.
* It needs to be sturdy (some fly well only once).
* It should be fairly simple to construct, so my seven-year-old can make it with little help (he should be able to make one that flies, so easy folding that results in good symmetry is important).
* It should require no scissors, tape, glue, or paper clips.

1 Fold an 8.5 x 11 sheet of paper in half, then unfold it. With the valley side face up, fold the top corners down to the center crease, figure 1.

2 Fold the top down at the base of the triangle. Then fold up about 1 inch of the tip, and unfold, figure 2.

3 Fold the top corners down so they meet in the center, just above the fold you created with the tip, figure 3. This leaves you with a blunt edge for the nose of the plane.

4 Fold the tip back up, over the corners, figure 4.

5 Fold in half so that folds are on the outside, figure 5.

6 Fold the wings down along dotted line shown in figure 5.

figure 4

figure 5

figure 6

Catch and Enjoy Fireflies

I t's still special and a little magical to me—that night in late spring or early summer when I first notice that the lightning bugs have begun to flash. I remember how thrilled I was to show them to Richard and teach him how to catch and save them in a jar. They are one of nature's very simple pleasures.

WHAT YOU'LL NEED
bug container or jar with holes punched in the lid
bug net (optional)
grass and twigs moistened with water

1 Go outside and wait for dusk.

2 Just as the sky begins to darken, look for fireflies rising from the grass and shrubs; you'll see them come out of the darkest, shadiest spots. Once they start coming out they are numerous, but after about thirty minutes they begin to peter out.

3 When you see one light up, go to where the flash was and wait for it to flash again. All you have to do is cup your hands around it and chances are you'll catch it. Or use a bug net. Fireflies basically land on the net as it goes by them.

4 Carefully place them in the jar, and put in some moist grass and twigs. Your children can bring them to their bedrooms and watch them glow while they fall asleep.

5 Be sure to release them the next morning.

65

Catch Worms

S o you've made your worm home, see page 91, but where are the worms? You know they come out when it's rainy and dark, though probably not for the reason you think. It isn't because they might drown in the water-rich soil. Because it's wet and overcast, they can emerge without getting dried out. You can take advantage of this if you need worms.

Saturate a patch of dirt with water, cover it with a dark trash bag, wait about an hour, and see whether any worms don't come to the surface.

SUPER TIP

Save extra photos for future use. There will be plenty of times that the kids will need pictures for school projects (eg. a timeline of their life). Store them in a small box with dividers for each year. This will make it easy to find what you are looking for.

—CAROLYN, MOM OF DELIA AND DANNY

Show Flowers Blooming

Find a plant whose flower opens at a given time and so quickly that even a three-year-old has the patience to watch and appreciate the magic of a flower blooming. Common evening primrose and moonflower are both good choices. Each flower blooms in the evening, because the plant is pollinated at night, and closes the next morning.

The yellow primrose flowers grow in bunches at the end of the stalklike plant. The flowers are numerous, so if your little one strays before the show begins, there will be plenty of opportunity to watch them as they literally burst open one by one. Here in New Jersey they flower in July and August. Showtime is around eight o'clock in the evening.

Primroses are easy-to-grow biennials, producing flowers in their second year, and can be found throughout most of the United States. I discovered them accidentally. They came in a package of wildflower seed, which I planted around my yard. I recall Richard watching them open. We went out evening after evening to witness it. I think it was one of his earliest exposures to the wonders of nature, which continues to amaze him to this day.

Make Telephones

Here is a fun activity that can also be a learning experience, because working with sound is a science project. Sound is a vibration so the noise will travel only as well as the quality of the instruments you are using. Therefore, you'll need to use cups that can vibrate or move.

WHAT YOU'LL NEED
2 paper or light plastic cups
scissors
about 50 feet of kite string or dental floss
2 paper clips

1 Poke a small hole in the bottom of the cups with the point of the scissors.

2 Thread the string through each hole and tie the string around the paper clip on the inside of each cup so the string doesn't slip out.

3 Have two kids each take a cup and move apart from each other until the string is straight and taut between them. Then they can talk to one another.

68

Use a Yo-Yo

Really cheap yo-yos, like the kind you get in goody bags, just don't work well, and your child will likely get frustrated attempting to use them. But that doesn't mean you'll have to pay more than five dollars for a yo-yo that's good enough for your child to learn with.

1 First get the string length correct. When the yo-yo is at the floor and the string is around the finger, it should come roughly to the belly button.

2 The string should be secured with a slipknot to the middle finger on the dominant hand, between the first and second joint.

3 It is best for beginners if the string is attached to the yo-yo with a double loop, figure 1. This way the yo-yo doesn't spin at the bottom and comes back up more easily. If the yo-yo is attached with a single loop, figure 2,

figure 1

figure 2

untwist the string by spinning the yo-yo counterclockwise until the string splits in two, then wrap it around the axle a second time.

4 To throw the yo-yo first hold it in your hand palm up, your middle finger aligned with the axle. The sting should come across the top of the yo-yo to your finger, figure 3. Now bend your elbow with your hand at your shoulder as if making a muscle. Release the yo-yo by quickly bringing your hand down and flicking your wrist so the yo-yo rolls off the ends of your fingers. As the yo-yo reaches the end of the string, turn your hand palm down and lift slightly. The yo-yo should come back up to your hand.

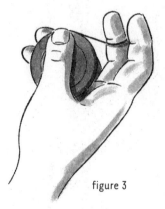

figure 3

69

Entertain for Free (practically)

There are times when you just need to get out of the house, and you don't have a lot of money or patience for a museum. Besides the library, the playground, and the mall, there are a number of places you can take your kids at very little or no cost. I have learned a few over the years.

✳ My neighbor Trish, told me how she would take her boys to **construction sites** where they could watch the big trucks working, either from the car or from a safe distance. I've done this, along with watching house demolition and house construction. All have proven to be entertaining.

✳ My friend Lisa told me that she would take her son to the **car wash**, sometimes even when the car didn't need it, just because he loved to sit in the car while it was washed. This has occasionally given my kids a welcome diversion.

✳ A trip to a **commuter train station** is very entertaining. I learned this when my husband and I both worked and we picked each other up at the train station. Now it's one of John's favorite things. Sometimes the kids are so entertained that it's hard to get them back in the car. You might even take a short trip, just one stop. On our train line, kids under twelve travel free.

✶ Then, of course, there is always a walk past the **firehouse**, just to look at the fire engines. Or if you live close to a small airport, you might be able to park someplace close enough that you could safely watch the planes take off.

✶ On Saturday mornings my friend Donna and her neighbors head to the **high school track**. The kids ride their bikes around the track (or roller-blade) while the parents walk and chat. Plus, the kids can play soccer on the nearby fields.

✶ Donna also takes her son to **bookstores** and reads to him. She gets to have a cup of coffee and, by the time they're done with a few books, he has usually picked out one that he prefers over the others.

✶ She's also willing to take her son to a toy store on a Sunday and let him pick out one small toy, but she also allows him to play with whatever he wants while they're in the store. Once again, after an hour playing with everything, he usually doesn't care that they don't go home with the biggest toy available.

Colorful Snow Angels

When it snows, you can always tell which houses have kids and which don't. The magic stillness of freshly fallen snow doesn't last long. Once the snowsuits, hats, gloves, and boots are wrestled into duty, it's all over and the fun begins. There are snowmen, snow forts, snowball fights, and the resulting mess of footprints. Snow angels are best made before the carpet of snow has been disturbed.

WHAT YOU'LL NEED
snow
squirt or spray bottles
water
food coloring

1 To make the snow angels, lie on your back in the snow and drag your outstretched arms up and down, from your head to your waist to make the wings. Then open and shut your legs to make the body.

2 You can make a few in a row, right next to one another, like they are holding hands. Or you can make them in a circle and create a ring of angels. For different sizes you can have everyone in the family make his or her own angel.

3 If you want to color them, fill some squirt bottles with water and add food coloring before you leave the house.

4 Squirt the angels with the colored water. If you made a string of them you can spray each one a different color. Or you can color the wings, the dress, and the head with different colors.

Make Edible Jewelry

This jewelry is like those candy necklaces that are loaded with sugar, but you can make them out of any small food with a hole in the middle.

✻ String together some Cheerios or Fruit Loops to make a necklace or a bracelet. A shoelace, dental floss or even licorice will make a good string.

✻ In the summer when it's really hot, you can make a necklace out of ice cubes for older kids. Start with a clean shoelace that is long enough to fit over your child's head when tied. Fill an ice cube tray with water and lay the shoelace into it so that it is suspended in each cube of water. Put it in the freezer. When it is frozen, carefully remove the cubes from the tray. Hang it around your child's neck and tie it. For bracelets, use smaller laces with just a few cubes. You can use patterned or colorful shoelaces to make them more fun.

72

Make a Paper Boat (and hat)

Fortunately, when I needed to make a paper boat and couldn't, I knew exactly where to look: Curious George Rides a Bike, pages 17–18, when George makes a fleet of paper boats out of the newspapers he's supposed to be delivering.

figure 1

1 Fold an 8.5 x 11-inch sheet of paper in half so the crease is widthwise.

2 With the folded edge at top, fold it in half widthwise, then open it, figure 1.

figure 2

3 Fold down both top corners along the center crease to form triangles, figure 2.

figure 3

4 Fold up the top layer of the remaining strip along the bottom.

figure 4

5 Turn the paper over and fold up the remaining strip on that side. (This is the aforementioned hat, figure 3.)

6 Hold each side at the bottom of the center crease and pull them apart, figure 4, so the points of the triangle come together to form a flat diamond shape.

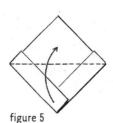

figure 5

7 Fold the bottom half of the diamond up on one side, then fold up the other side, figure 5. You are left with a triangle.

8 Hold each side at the bottom of the center crease and pull them apart so the points come together to form a flat diamond shape, figure 6.

figure 6

9 At the top, pull the outer layers of paper out, away from each other, figure 7, to form the "boat." The inner layer will peak up to form the "sail," figure 8.

figure 7

figure 8

73

Paint Tee Shirts

Kids love to paint on clothing, it's like permission to
make a mess. This is a fun activity
for parties.

WHAT YOU'LL NEED
acrylic paint
various types of spray bottles
(different bottles will give
varied effects)
water
white clothing to paint (tee
shirts, socks, sneakers, hats)

1 Fill spray bottles about ½
to ⅔ full with paint and dilute
with water. It should be just
thin enough to spray through
the nozzle.

2 Insert a plastic bag inside
shirts and socks so the color
doesn't bleed through to
other side.

3 Prop or hang items on a
tree or fence.

4 Let the kids spray the items
with a few colors creating
unique designs.

5 Let dry completely.

Catch "Sand Crabs"

Mole crabs (or "sand crabs," a common misnomer) can be found along the Atlantic coast from Cape Cod to Florida as well as in Texas. The Pacific variety is found along the coast from Alaska to Baja California. With just a bucket a child can be entertained for hours.

The best place to dig is in the wet sand between the high and low waterline. Look for bubbles coming up out of the sand as the water washes back. While you dig with your hands watch and feel for the crabs burrowing through the sand. Gently place them in the bucket with sand and water. Don't worry; they don't bite. For the grand finale, dump the bucket in the wet sand and watch them all scurry and burrow back into the sand. Make sure they all make it back; you don't want any to get stuck in the dry sand, where they will die.

SUPER TIP

Give your kids some catalogs or magazines and let them rip out pictures. If they are old enough you can give them scissors, glue and paper to make a collage.

—DONNA, MOM OF JAMES

75

Make a Flower Crown

Little girls love to be a princesses. Late summer, when black-eyed Susans bloom in bunches, is a great time to for them to be a fairy princesses with a crown of flowers. You can use any type of flower with a long enough stem that is not too stiff.

1 Cut a bunch of flowers with a 3- to 5-inch stem. The denser the crown and the bigger the kid's head, the more flowers you'll need. I found that twenty was enough for my four-year-old's average-size head.

2 Remove any leaves from the stem, so you have a clean stem with a flower on the end. Keep your flowers in water while you work to keep them fresh.

3 Poke a ¼- to ½-inch slit in the stem of one flower with your thumbnail or a knife. The closer to the flower that you make the slit the denser your crown will be and the more flowers you'll need. A space of 1 to 2 inches gives a nice density.

4 Thread the stem of the next flower through the slit. Pull it all the way through so the flower is at the slit.

5 Twist the stems together once or twice, then cut a slit in the second stem. Thread a third flower through the second slit. Twist the second and third stems around the first. Cut a slit in the third stem. Thread the fourth flower through the third slit. Twist the third and fourth stems around the other stems. Cut a slit in the fourth stem.

6 Continue cutting a slit, threading, and then twisting the last two stems around the rest until your chain is long enough.

7 Cut a longer slit in the last stem and carefully slip the first flower through the slit.

8 Carefully weave the stems at the end into the stems at the beginning to secure your ring.

76

Make a Paper Helicopter

This paper helicopter or whirligig is great because it is so simple. The key, I have found, is not too much wind and the right weight paper. The typical printer paper is a bit too light, but card stock works well. The added weight of a paper clip at the bottom helps the flight.

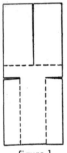

figure 1

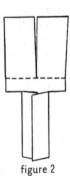

figure 2

WHAT YOU'LL NEED

scissors
8.5 x 11-inch sheet of paper
ruler
paper clip

1 Cut the paper into equal thirds widthwise. Each third will make one helicopter.

2 Using one of the pieces of paper, measure and cut a 3¾-inch-long slit lengthwise down the middle, figure 1.

3 Measure ¾ inch from the end of the slit and draw a horizontal rule across the width of the paper. Measure 1 inch in from each side of the

paper and draw vertical lines
from the rule to the bottom
of the paper, figure 1.

4 Cut 1-inch slits into each
side of the paper along the
horizontal rule. Fold the two
sides in along the vertical
lines, figure 2.

5 Fold the bottom edge up
about ¾ inch. Secure with a
paper clip.

6 At the top, fold the two
halves down to opposite sides
so they stick out perpendicular to the bottom, figure 3.
These are the propellers.

7 Hold the helicopter from
the bottom. With your arm
held your arm straight up,
give it a slight push upward,
and let it spin down.

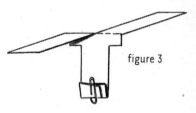

figure 3

Make Tracks in the Snow

K ids enjoy identifying animal tracks in the snow. But since most of us only live near birds, squirrels, and rabbits, you can make your own more exotic tracks. Remember, you don't have to stick to animals—dinosaurs had feet, too, and most small children are fascinated by those prehistoric creatures!

WHAT YOU'LL NEED
heavy cardboard
scissors
rubber bands or shoelaces

1 Draw the shapes of different animal prints on cardboard, making them slightly larger than your child's foot.

2 Cut them out and put a small hole on each side.

3 Attach them to her boot with a rubber band or shoelaces.

4 Let her walk around in the snow. You can make various prints and have her guess what animal it is.

Make an Ant Farm

Any mom who keeps a jar of ants in her home is already a supermom. I feel as if the little buggers are crawling on me just writing about it ... so if you're willing to keep ants in your house, consider yourself a hero already.

WHAT YOU'LL NEED

full soda can

large jar (large peanut butter jars are a good shape)

some dirt

moist sponge or cotton ball

some ants (collect them from the same anthill or they will fight each other)

piece of fabric large enough to fit over the mouth of the jar

rubber band

black construction paper

tape

pieces of fruit, bread dipped in sugar water, or dry pet food crumbs

1 Place the soda can in the center of the jar. And fill the space between the can and the jar with lightly packed dirt.

2 Put a piece of moist sponge on top of the soda can. Keep the sponge moist by removing it as needed, wetting it, and squeezing out the excess.

3 Put the ants in the dirt.

4 Cover the top of the jar with fabric and secure it tightly with the rubber band so the ants can't escape.

5 Wrap the black construction paper around the jar and tape it together. You can slide the paper off to observe the ants. It may take a while before you see tunnels.

6 Feed the ants some crumbs every few days.

A Pocket Garden

According to Richard, he coined the phrase "pocket garden." I picked him up from camp and he told me he'd made a pocket garden. I thought it was a project all the campers did. I imagined a small garden tucked away someplace. "It's a pocket garden because it fits in my pocket," he explained.

He picked up a plastic soda bottle cap in which he'd placed dirt and a small clover plant. Now, it sits on our front stoop along with his rock collection and his bug terrarium. This simple project can help your child notice and differentiate some of the tiny plants that grow, potentially gaining some appreciation for the diversity and fragility of the environment underfoot.

SUPER TIP

Use clear storage boxes with lids attached & handles for storing toys with many pieces. Toys are easy to identify because the containers are clear. They can be stacked and easily transported to sleep overs at grandma's.

—CAROLYN, MOM OF DELIA AND DANNY

Make Stilts From Cans

Kids really enjoy the challenge of walking on stilts. You can purchase stilts pretty inexpensively, but you can make them yourself for even less.

WHAT YOU'LL NEED
two cans
heavy tape
can opener
length of rope
scissors

1 Save two of the same type cans, coffee cans work well. Many now open without can openers and don't have sharp edges. If the cans do have sharp edges put heavy tape over them and don't let toddlers play with them.

2 With a can opener, puncture two holes at the base (not the bottom) of each can on opposite sides.

3 Run a thin rope through the holes and tie the ends together. The top of the loop should be roughly at the waist.

4 Have your child step one foot onto each can. As he walks, he should use the rope to keep his feet in position on the can and to guide the cans. To help balance he should stand up straight and not look down at his feet.

ACTIVITY | ✿

Catch Bugs (without using your hands)

Kids are sometimes so excited about picking up bugs that they crush them. It's difficult for them to be as gentle as they need to be with such small creatures. A great solution for this is a hands-free bug catcher. Don't forget a magnifying glass for close inspection of your new pets.

WHAT YOU'LL NEED
scissors
cardboard
clean jar with a wide opening
2 pieces of plastic tubing
(about 6 and 15 inches long)
very thin fabric or fine netting
rubber band
tape
clay

1 Cut a circle of cardboard the size of the jar's opening. Poke two holes in the cardboard the size of the tubing.

2 Slip the tubes through the holes. Fasten a small piece of fabric to the end of the shorter tube with a rubber band.

3 Tape the cardboard to the jar so that two ends of tubing (one of which is covered) are in the jar.

4 Seal any gaps around the tubes with clay.

5 To catch bugs, place the end of the longer piece of tubing over the insect and suck on the shorter end.

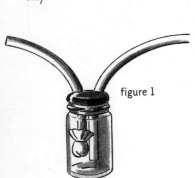

figure 1

Trace a Footpath

I spend a lot of time on the street with my kids attempting to have a conversation with another adult, so I should have many suggestions for keeping the kids occupied while the adults talk, but I don't. The following idea comes from my neighbor Lisa. I thought this was brilliant.

One day when we were trying to talk, I gave the kids a bucket of street chalk. That only led to requests for us to draw this or that. Lisa gave them each a piece of chalk and had them trace around her feet as she took small steps. They took turns tracing her feet, first the left, then the right, and so on. They created a path from her door to ours. More kids joined in to color each footstep with his or her own design.

SUPER TIP

Keep bubble wrap (in a safe spot as plastic is a choking hazard.) Jumping on it will provide an outlet for excess energy.

—JOELLEN, MOM OF PETER AND LAURA

Create a Rock Collection

Richard, like many boys, loves to collect rocks. Perhaps it is the influence of his father, who majored in geology in college. This project is perfect for the budding geologist. You can help him learn about the rocks he finds by bringing him to the library or bookstore to get books about rock collecting and identifying.

WHAT YOU'LL NEED

an egg carton
8 small boxes
(soap or Jell-o boxes)
pencil and paper
scissors
a stapler or glue
cotton
water and a toothbrush
acetate or plastic wrap

1 To start your child can collect various rocks and sort them in the egg cartons.

2 Then he can make small labels for the rocks, writing down when and where they were found as well as the type of rock.

MAKE A DISPLAY BOX

1 Lay the eight small boxes flat and cut off the tops.

2 Glue or staple the sides of the boxes together in two rows of four.

3 Fill each box with cotton.

4 Your child can clean his very best specimens with water and a toothbrush and place them in the box with a label when they are dry.

5 Cover the display with plastic wrap or a piece of acetate.

84

Trace Bodies

This can be done on the sidewalk or in the driveway with chalk or, for something more permanent, on a large sheet of craft paper. If you don't have craft paper, cut open some big paper bags and staple or tape them together to make a really big sheet of heavy paper.

1 Have your child lie down on the paper and trace his body with a bold magic marker.

2 Then set him free to decorate himself with chalk (if the image is on the sidewalk) or with crayons, paint, yarn, construction paper, magazine pictures, or whatever you have (if the image is on paper).

SUPER TIP

When you're outside doing yard work on a warm day, give the kids a bucket of water with soap and have them wash their swings or the patio furniture.

—JACQUI, MOM OF JOHN, EMILY, LAURA AND DECLAN

Raise Tadpoles

Down the street from the house where I grew up was a stream. In early summer, bunches of tadpoles were swimming around in the stream (check the timing in your own area) and by late summer, frog spotting was a popular activity for the neighborhood kids. Where I live now there is a wooded area with a pond and stream nearby. Richard wanted to observe how a tadpole turns into a frog. Given the rapidly declining frog population, I was surprised when we discovered that there were, in fact, tadpoles living in the nearby pond. After doing some research to make sure we weren't endangering the tadpoles, we decided to catch a couple so we could observe them as they transformed.

WHAT YOU'LL NEED
net or bucket
fish tank or fishbowl
pond water
algae from pond or lettuce
rock
tadpoles

1 Prepare the fish tank with pond water for the tadpoles. A fish aquarium works well. Make sure it contains no soap or chemical residue. Fill it with water from the same pond where you will get the tadpoles. Place a decent-size rock on the bottom. You should not have more than two tadpoles per gallon of water. Keep your tank out of direct sunlight in a spot that is cool.

2 The water in the tank needs to be changed with fresh pond water and the tank cleaned (do not use soap or chemicals) at least every three days, sooner if it begins to look dirty. Do not use tap water; the chemicals added to tap water could kill the tadpoles.

3 Catch the tadpoles with a net or a bucket and bring them home in the bucket with some pond water.

4 You can feed them with fresh algae from the pond or give them chopped-up lettuce that has been boiled for fifteen minutes. (You can store the boiled lettuce in the freezer.) Feed them a pinch of lettuce every day. If the lettuce sits around for a while, give them less because it will make the water dirty. If the lettuce goes quickly, give them a little more. If the tadpoles don't have enough to eat they will go after each other.

5 Over the course of a few weeks (depending on the tadpoles' species and age when caught), they will begin to change into frogs. They will develop small bumps, which will become back legs, then they will develop front legs. The tail gradually disappears. They will stop eating while this happens. Also, you will begin to notice that the mouth becomes more frog-like. The rock is important when they begin to develop lungs and breathe air.

6 This is a good time to release your frogs at the pond where you originally got them.

86

Make a Parachute (for toys)

I recall the day I found Richard and his friend outside with tissues and dental floss, making parachutes for their action figures. The tissues kept ripping and the tape they were using to attach everything wasn't working. Together we came up with a better parachute using an old fabric napkin. You can use any fabric square, the lighter the better.

WHAT YOU'LL NEED
a square of light fabric
needle and thread
a small action figure

1 Use the needle to attach a strand of thread through each corner of the napkin. Each strand should be the same length.

2 Tie the threads to the action figure.

SUPER TIP

On a nice day bring a blanket and a basket of toys outside and let your child play with them there. It seems exciting to them!

—DONNA, MOM NICHOLAS AND CARTER

Make an Igloo

I guess by definition this isn't actually an igloo; it's more like a snow cave. But it'll probably be a lot faster and much less frustrating to build. Besides, no one is going to live in it—it's supposed to be fun. Never leave children alone while tunneling in the snow or playing in the cave; collapsed snow could suffocate a child. Also, don't burn anything inside your cave unless you have a hole in the top for ventilation.

WHAT YOU'LL NEED
a lot of snow
some shovels
a garden hose connected to a water source
freezing or below freezing temperatures.

1 Pack down a big pile of snow.

2 Spray it with water and let it freeze overnight.

3 The next day, use shovels to break through where the entrance will be and start hollowing it out.

4 Once it is complete, you can smooth over the inside walls to get them to ice over.

88

Play Hopscotch

I considered this an outdoor game until I had children and realized the importance of indoor rainy day activities. I bought an indoor foam puzzle hopscotch set, but you could easily paint one on a rug like my baby sitter did, or tape it out on the floor.

1 First draw the pattern, figure 1, on the pavement with chalk. Next, each player picks a playing piece, such as a stone, beanbag, or bottle cap.

figure 1

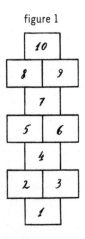

2 Throw your playing piece onto square one, then hop over square one and into squares two and three, one foot in each square. Continue by hopping with one foot in the single squares and two feet in the side-by-side squares, one in each square. When you reach square ten, turn around and hop back to squares two and three, where you stop, pick up your playing piece, hop over square one, and hop off the court. (Kids who can't manage hopping from one foot to two can hop however they want.)

3 Throw your playing piece onto square two, and continue on until you either misstep or miss the square when you throw. When you miss, leave your playing piece in the square you will attempt on your next turn. Players can't step on any squares that contain a playing piece.

figure 2

4 The players take turns and play continues until someone wins by completing the jumps through square ten.

figure 3

✳ Alternative hopscotch patterns are the snail , figure 2, and the ladder, figure 3.

✳ Another game is to simply hop; first in each space with two feet, then on one foot, then on the other foot, and last on alternating feet.

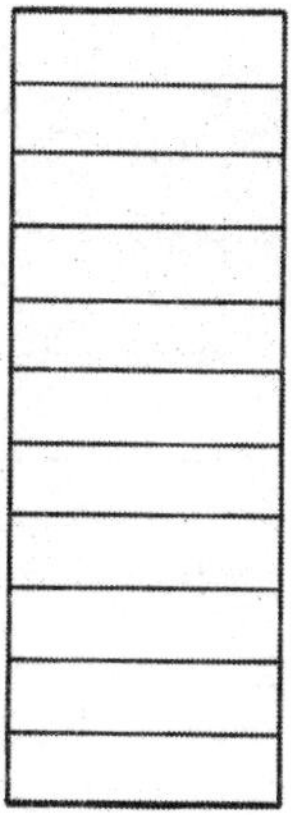

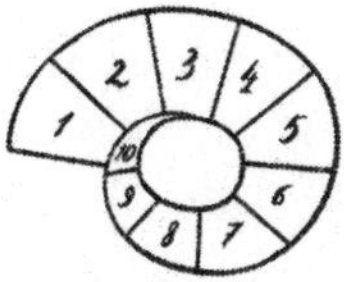

Play Dodge Ball

There are so many variations on this game, and you probably know one of them. When I was young we played this way: Two players stood about 50 feet apart from one another. The rest of the kids (as few as one or as many as you had) stood in the middle. The two kids on the ends threw the ball, trying to hit one of the kids in the middle. If someone got hit, she was out. The last player in the middle was the winner.

COMMON VARIATIONS

1 Players divide into two teams. One team forms a circle around the other. The team tries to eliminate the players in the center one at a time by tagging them, on the legs, with the ball. The last player in the middle is the winner. If a player gets hit above the waist, the person who threw the ball must sit out the rest of the game. If a player in the middle catches the ball before if bounces, the player who threw it is out.

2 The throwers stand in two lines facing each other while the other team runs around between them. When a player gets hit he joins the throwers. The last player in the middle is the winner.

3 Another way is to play on a rectangular court, such as a tennis court with no net. Each team moves around on their side. The players attempt to hit kids on the other team with the ball. When a player is out, she either leaves the game field or sits where she was tagged.

90

Play Punch Buggy

Now, you might regret teaching your kids this—they probably fight enough in the backseat of the minivan as it is—but I believe it's okay for kids to see their moms let loose once in a while, and this is a good car game for when the kids' energy is really pent up.

1 Point out Volkswagen Beetles to your kids.

2 Tell them that the first person who sees one is allowed to gently punch the shoulder of another nearby child for seeing the "bug."

3 As your kids become more adept at recognizing and distinguishing cars, you can expand the game:
    Dragon Wagon (you can roar)
    Convertible (mess up the other kid's hair)
    Truck Luck (blow a raspberry)
    Cuss Bus (allow the kids to pick out their own "bad" words; anything with fart, pee, and poop will usually make them happy)

Have a Snowball Fight

Kids love a good snowball fight, but for a really good battle, you first need a couple of forts—and some ground rules, such as no throwing at faces.

1 Decide the distance the forts should be from on another based on the throwing ability of the kids who will be battling. A good shape for forts is a "V" or a "C."

2 To build the fort, pile blocks or balls of snow on top of each other to create walls. You can roll out your own balls like you would to make a snowman (see page 168), or you can use the big chunks left on the side of the road by the snow plow and along the sidewalk from your shovel. Put the big pieces down first and the smaller pieces toward the top. It only needs to be tall enough so your child can crouch down to protect himself from incoming snowballs and still be able to stand and easily throw snowballs over the top.

3 You can use loose snow and small chunks to stabilize the wall and to fill in gaps. Leave some gaps as loopholes so the kids can see their opponents.

4 Before starting the battle, make lots of snowballs. Then get into position and start the battle. With a fort and the ammo at the ready, they can have a strategic game to see who gets the most hits.

Milk Container Scoops

Create ball scoops from gallon milk jugs; they're easy to make, and there always seems to be a couple of milk containers in the recycling bin. It's a great project if your child hasn't mastered catching yet. Toss the ball into his scoop and watch his face light up with pride over his accomplishment. Kids will also enjoy wearing them as hats or using them as megaphones.

* Wash the jugs and cut off the bottoms. Make sure the edges aren't sharp; if they are, you may need to put masking or electical tape over them.

* Grab a ball and you are ready to play.

SUPER TIP

Let your children "help" with chores. Give them a rag to dust, a broom to sweep, socks to sort, nonbreakable dishes to wash. They will enjoy the responsibilty and won't be making a mess.

—NINA, MOM OF MICHAEL, PEGGY, DON AND NICK

93

Play Marbles

My father had a jar of marbles up on a shelf in our basement. I loved to examine the colors and patterns. Later, they intrigued me because they were my dad's when he was a kid. I could just picture my father and my uncle as children playing marbles. I have a tin of marbles in my kitchen, it includes my own, my dad's, and my kids'. There are many games that can be played with marbles. The most common, ringer, is probably somewhat familiar.

1 Draw a 10-foot-wide circle. (With younger players you can make a smaller circle.) Draw two parallel lines touching the circle on opposite sides. Each player has a marble, usually a larger one, which is his shooter.

2 To determine which player starts the game, the players "lag" from one line to the other across the ring. To lag, a player tosses his shooter to the other line, or "knuckles down." To "knuckle down" means that you hold your hand in a fist, with a marble in the crook of your index finger and your thumb underneath the marble, figure 1. You must rest a knuckle on the ground to shoot. The child whose shooter comes nearest the line goes first.

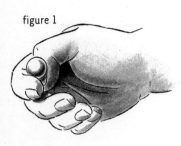

figure 1

3 At the start of the game, arrange thirteen marbles in an "X" on the center axis of the circle, one marble in the center and three on each leg, 3 inches apart from one another.

4 The first player "knuckles down" from any position around the ring. If the player knocks a marble from the ring, he keeps the marble and goes again. If no marble goes out of the ring it's the next player's turn.

5 A player can shoot at any of the marbles, including the other player's shooter.

6 If she aims for the shooter and knocks it out of ring, she wins all the marbles the player has taken and that player is out of the game.

7 If a player's shooter stops in the ring at his next turn, he "knuckles down" inside the ring where his shooter stopped. Players can't step inside the ring unless their shooter comes to a stop inside the ring. The penalty for stepping into the ring unnecessarily is a fine of one marble.

8 The game is over when there are no more marbles in the ring. The player with the most marbles wins. If it has been predetermined that the game is being played for keeps, each player keeps the marbles he or she has won. If not, all the marbles are returned to their original owners.

94

Play Kick the Can

We live on a very low traffic block with ten houses. There are twelve kids (mostly boys) between the ages of two and twelve (plus a few younger and a few older). Kick the can has been very popular with them for the past couple of years. Traditionally, it's just a variation on hide and seek. In our neighborhood, it has evolved into a variation on tag. It's all about getting to or guarding the can. The can, simple as it is, makes the game significantly more exciting to the kids. I love that something so simple can make such a big difference. Here are the Woodside Road rules according to Max (with help from Sam, Hugo, and Richard).

WHAT YOU'LL NEED

can
some playing space
a group of three or more kids
(the more the better)

1 Prior to the start of the game a stoop or tree may be designated a "safe spot."

2 Someone is the guard.

3 The players disperse while the guard counts to fifty.

4 The guard chases the players in an effort to tag them or the guard hovers around the can while the other players attempt to kick it without being tagged. If the guard tags a player, he or she is out.

5 If a player kicks the can, the game starts again and that player is the guard.

6 When everyone is out, the guard is "it" again. After two turns of being "it," the guard chooses someone else.

The game is traditionally played with these rules:

* The players hide.
* There isn't a "safe spot."
* When the guard finds someone, they race to the can to see who can kick it first. If the guard gets there first, the player is out; if the hider gets there first, the hider is "it" and the game starts again.
* A player may come out of his hiding place and kick the can, before being spotted, to free the players who are out. They may then rejoin the game.

SUPER TIP

A playful routine for getting kids to cooperate after their bath is to wrap them in a towel and pretend they're a package. Open it and there's a cute puppy. After the puppy crawls around, begin to "groom" it: brush its "fur," "check" its teeth, and put on its "doggy sweater."

—BETH, MOM OF LAUREN AND BAILEY

Play SPUD

This is another great game that will make you seem super-cool to the kids in your neighborhood. I have no idea why it's called SPUD, though.

1 The kids stand in a group and count off so each one has a number.

2 The person who is "it" throws the ball up in the air and calls out a number. Everyone runs except the person whose number was called. That player catches the ball. Once he has caught it, he calls out, "SPUD," and the other players must stop in their tracks.

3 The player with the ball spells out S-P-U-D as he takes one step with each letter. From that position he may attempt to tag the closest player with the ball. The player he is attempting to tag may move his body but not his feet to avoid the ball.

4 If the player is tagged he gets an "S" and becomes "it." If the ball misses the player, the thrower gets an "S" and is "it" again.

5 Players are eliminated when they have S, P, U, and D. The last player in the game wins.

GAME

Play Chinese Jumprope

I have fond memories of playing Chinese jump rope in my back-yard. I have a sister a year older than me, and we had a mutual friend a year older than my sister. We did everything together. As you can imagine, there were times when three was one too many kids. But for Chinese jump rope, we were just right.

WHAT YOU'LL NEED
A Chinese jump rope (looks like a circular bungee cord)

1 Two players stand a few feet apart, facing each other, with the jump rope around their ankles and taut between them, figure 1. The third player completes a sequence of jumps (described below). If the jumper makes a mistake, she stops and another player takes a turn.

figure 1

figure 2

figure 3

figure 4

2 To start, jump into the middle of the ropes with both feet, figure 2.

3 Next, jump so you are straddling one side of the rope, figure 3. From this position, jump so the outside foot is in the middle and the inside foot is on the opposite side. Jump side to side four times.

4 Jump back into the middle of the rope. From there, jump to the outside of the rope so you are straddling both sides of the rope, figure 4.

5 Jump into the middle again and then jump onto the rope so one foot lands on each side of the rope, figure 5.

6 Then jump out to one side of the rope.

7 Place your feet under the rope and jump across so you pull it over the other side, figure 6. Jump out of the triangle and do it again in the other direction.

figure 5

8 Do the first half of the previous move (step 7), but instead of jumping out once the rope is crossed over, push the straight rope out with one ankle so the rope forms a diamond around your ankles, figure 7. To finish, jump out of that position and straddle the ropes.

figure 6

9 As you become more experienced, and to increase the challenge, repeat the sequence of jumps with the rope at the players' knees and then their waists. (I never got beyond my ankles.)

figure 7

97

Fly a Kite

Kite flying is one of those things that all parents end up having to do with their kids, but that few of them really know how to do well, so they rely on luck to get the kite high enough to impress their kids and make it a worthwhile outing. However, you don't need to rely on luck, these few steps should get your kite way up high in just a few minutes.

HERE ARE SOME TIPS TO START OUT:

1 Get the right kite; the delta is a good one for beginners.

2 Find an area to fly it without obstructions and away from roads, airplanes, trees, and power lines. The beach or an open field in a park is always good.

3 Pick a good day that has some wind but not too much; somewhere between 5 and 15 mph is good for deltas. Never fly a kite in rain or in thunder and lightening storms.

4 Bring a small repair kit, just in case: scissors, tape, and some extra string.

5 Know the basics of the kite and have at least a simple explanation for why it flies:

The cover, or sail, is the material that catches the wind. The frame, or spars, supports the sail. The bridle is the strings (or string) that attach the kite to the flying line. The tail adds stability. The wind pushes against the sail of the kite. The kite can't go with the wind because it is attached to the line, and this creates drag. As you hold the line, you pull the spars. This angles the kite into the wind, forcing the wind to pass over and under it and creating what in aerodynamic terms is called lift, or an upward exerted force. The combination of drag and lift allows the kite to defy gravity and fly.

NOW YOU NEED TO GET THE KITE IN THE AIR:

Stand so the wind is at your back. Hold the kite up by the bridle with the bridle facing into the wind. Let out some line. The kite should take flight if there's enough wind. Let the kite fly a bit, then as the kite angles upward pull on the line to give it lift. Continue this as your kite gains altitude.

HERE'S HOW TO KEEP IT IN THE AIR:

As long as the kite is inclined upward you need to keep the line tight. If the kite begins to dive you need to loosen up on the line to allow the kite to right itself. Once it does, tighten the line again so it begins to climb.

YOU'LL ALSO NEED TO BRING IT BACK DOWN:

Allow some time to bring your kite in slowly. Don't wind the string too fast or the kite may crash.

Use a Hula Hoop

Last time I was at my childhood home, I noticed my parents still had my hula hoop in their basement. Sometimes when I'm down there with the kids, I pick it up and give it a go. If you leave some hula hoops lying around a group of adults it won't be long before they are all showing off their ability. I gave my daughter these important tips:

1 Start with the right size hoop. The hoop held up in front of you should rest on the floor and reach somewhere between your belly button and your nipple.

2 To get started, hold the hoop against your back and spin it around your body by throwing it to one side (whichever side works best for you).

3 To keep it going, stand with one foot in front of the other and thrust your hips forward and back, NOT around and around. Practice, practice, practice.

99

Read a Compass

A compass works because of Earth's magnetic field. The needle on a compass will always point to magnetic north, which is in the same direction, but not exactly the same place, as true north. Magnetic north is an unfixed northern point of Earth's polar magnetic force and is roughly several hundred miles away from the North Pole, or true north. These two points are close enough that, unless you are very far north, your compass will point generally in the direction of true north.

1 To read a compass you shouldn't be near anything metal.

2 Hold the compass still and level in front of you. Rotate it until the needle points to the spot marked north. Now south, east, and west are also properly aligned on the compass.

3 Once you determine the direction of your destination, you can realign your compass as you travel to make sure you continue in that direction.

SUPER TIP

Save things your child finds while on vacation, to make souvenirs, such as smooth rocks to paint and shells to make necklaces.

—LISA, MOM OF ALEX

100

Build a Sandcastle

Most people wonder why their fill-the-bucket, dump-the-bucket sand castles never look like the ones they see on the beach, abandoned by an architectural sand genius. As it turns out, there are some basic but critical things you need to know if you want to build a good sturdy sand castle.

1 First and foremost, water is as critical as sand when it comes to building a sand castle. The sand needs to be very wet. The water is what holds the sand together.

2 Second, packing the sand is critical. Packing allows the water to bind the sand.

3 Lastly, making patties and bricks with your hands is probably better than using pails and molds. Too often the sand sticks to the container when you dump it out.

4 Get wet sand by putting sand and water into a pail or by digging until you hit water. Pick a spot that isn't too close to the rising tide. I prefer a spot that is safe from the tide, but still near the surf, so I can dig up wet sand and haul water easily.

5 Make walls and towers using bricks and patties. Make walls by stacking bricks and make towers by stacking patties. Place larger patties on the bottom and make them gradually smaller as your tower gets taller.

6 When forming your bricks and patties, you should pack them well and use two hands. Shake them gently so the water gets into the sand before adding them to the tower.

7 Dribble more wet sand to bind the walls and towers together.

8 Once you've built the basic structure, smooth it out and then carve the details: crenels, windows, doors, steps, arches, and loopholes. You can buy special sand-sculpting tools or you can use plastic utensils, Popsicle sticks, and straws. Start at the top and work down.

9 Of course, three things that you need to make your castle one of the aforementioned enviable structures are time, practice, and patience. But you're at the beach, and what else is there to do? Right kids? Kids?

101

Pump a Swing

Although a child can't do this until she is developmentally able, some pointers will help her understand how to use her body correctly.

1 When pushing your child, tell her that as the swing goes forward she should hold her legs straight out in front. As the swing goes backward, she should tuck her legs under the swing. As I pushed Anita, we would sing together, "Out, under, out, under ..." I found that once she was able to maintain that motion, the key was teaching her to use her upper body and arms.

2 First make sure your child always holds on with both hands. Then explain that she should lean her upper body

figure 1

back slightly when the swing is all the way back. As the swing moves forward, she should pull her body up toward the chains using her arms. When the swing goes all the way back, she should lean her body back again.

3 In this coordinated motion of the legs, arms, and upper body, the child transitions from a somewhat reclined position (swinging forward), figure 1 to an upright, seated position (swinging backward) figure 2. As the child gets older, the movement becomes more fluid and she can lean back more and pull forward more strongly to get the swing going high and fast.

figure 2

Win at Carnival Games

Believe it or not, state fairs rake in about $60 million each year just from people trying to win prizes. But you can be a sucker no more. Here's how to win those stuffed animals! The first rule is to play group games with everyone in the family; this way someone will win.

POPPING A BALLOON WITH A DART

Stand around and watch a few games. The balloons that have survived some games are more likely to pop sooner rather than later. Check the darts. If they're dull, ask for another set. Dull darts can't pop balloons.

GETTING THE BASKETBALL IN THE HOOP OR THE DIME IN THE GLASS

This is a tough one to win, because the hoop and the ball often aren't regulation size—the hoop isn't truly round and the ball is overinflated. If you try it, don't rely on the backboard for help. Instead, try to drop the ball straight into the hoop. The dime will slide off the crystal glasses, so toss it in a high arc and avoid hitting the edge of the glassware.

SHOOTING WITH A BB GUN

This is also a tough game, because you don't get that many pellets and the operators rig the sights so that you aren't really shooting straight (even though it seems like your aim is correct). Take some shots to see where the gun is truly aiming, and then adjust.

TOSSING A BALL INTO A BASKET

Toss very gently, because there is a bounce at the bottom of the basket.

CATAPULTING A FROG ONTO A LILY PAD

Do not aim for the closest lily pad! Those catapults can make a frog really hop. Instead, launch the frog as high and as hard as possible toward any lily pad—you can't really aim. Also, be sure to fold the frog's legs under its stomach (that's how the real frogs do it!).

103

Carve a Pumpkin

Since your kids can't do the actual carving, ask them to draw the face on a piece of paper so you can transfer their design to the jack-o'-lantern. Or check out books and online resources for more complicated patterns.

WHAT YOU'LL NEED
pumpkin
small serrated knife
large spoon
pin or nail
pumpkin-carving kit (optional)
candle or flashlight
paper
tape
flour
pencil (optional)
petroleum jelly

1 Select a pumpkin without scratches or bruises. If you know the pattern you want to carve select a size and shape that will accomodate it.

2 If you are doing a simple face you can get by with a small serrated knife, a large spoon, and a pin. If your design is intricate you should consider a pumpkin-carving kit, which comes with saws, scrapers, scoops, and pokers.

3 With the knife, cut a hole around the stem large enough for your spoon or hand to get inside and clean it out. Cut a hexagon shape angled in toward the center so the top doesn't fall through when you put it back on. Or you can cut the hole in the bottom and put the pumpkin over a candle—like a lampshade. But, you still need a small hole at the top so the heat can escape and the pumpkin won't dry out as quickly.

4 Clean out all the seeds-save them for eating or making jewelry (see page 177)—and scrape the sides to remove the pulp and strings. Scrape off enough pulp so the pumpkin is no more than an inch thick for easier carving. A clean, smooth interior will give a nice even glow. If you cut the hole at the top, dig a recess in the bottom to hold the candle or a small flashlight.

5 If your pattern is intricate, size it correctly on paper, leaving about a 1-inch border. Tape the paper to the pumpkin and with a pin, poke holes along the pattern into the skin of the pumpkin to create guidelines for carving. You can smooth flour over the holes to make

them easier to see when you're ready to carve. If your pattern is simple, you can draw it on the pumpkin with a pencil.

6 Cut the center parts of your pattern first. Use a slow, gentle, sawing motion. Making a lot of small cuts is better than making big cuts. Remove the biggest pieces last; if they are difficult to remove, cut them into smaller sections. Push the pieces out rather than in with your fingers.

7 To keep the pumpkin from drying out too quickly, coat the cut surfaces with petroleum jelly. If it does dry out, soak it in cold water for up to eight hours. If you need to preserve it for a long time you can keep it in the refrigerator wrapped in plastic.

Throw a Frisbee (backhand)

Guys are always impressed when a girl can throw a Frisbee well (at least the guys I dated). Not that that matters anymore—I married one of those guys and now I have to impress our kids. My secret for learning how to throw a Frisbee came from my oldest brother, Tom, who was on the Ultimate Frisbee team at Rutgers University (National Champions, 1973 to 1976). He wanted all our siblings to learn to throw well, so he could practice with us while he was home.

1 You need an appropriate-size disc for the child's strength. A disc that weighs 120 grams or less should work well. Brand names discs, such as Frisbee and those made by Discraft, fly better than other brands and state the weight on the package.

2 Pick a relatively calm day. Wind can be difficult for a weaker thrower to deal with.

3 The backhand throw is most efficiently made by a right-handed thrower who is facing ninety degrees left of

figure 1

the intended line of flight. The (right-handed) thrower starts with the disc near and just above the left hip.

4 The wrist of the hand holding the disc should curl up or flex toward the inside of the right elbow. By swinging the arm toward the intended line of flight and flipping the wrist out along that line, two or three nanoseconds later the thrower creates, respectively, forward momentum and spin of the disc. The faster it spins, the longer the disc's potential for continued flight.

5 Under most conditions, the angle of projection, at the release of the throw should be such that the edge of the Frisbee further away from the body is somewhat lower than the edge nearest the body. If it is too low, however, the disc will likely curve to the left. The thrower needs to experiment with the angle.

6 Another angle to consider is the degree to which the front, or leading edge, of the disc is above the tail, or trailing edge, as the disc begins its flight. The front needs to be higher than the back, figure 1, or it just won't work. The thrower needs to experiment with this angle as well.

7 Children are generally captivated by the physics of disc flight, which are very different than the trajectory of a ball.

105

Teach Kids to Ride a Bike

I distinctly remember the day I learned to ride a two-wheeled bike solo. My father held on to the back of the seat and ran alongside me, letting go when he felt I was ready. I proceeded up the street, went up the driveway, and headed straight for a tree.

This brings me to something my neighbor David said when I was teaching Anita (still on training wheels): "First show her how to use the brakes." Important stuff, but what every kid really needs to ride a bike is a sense of balance. This technique develops their sense of balance, results in less scrapes and bruises, and really works:

1 Find a grassy slope of about twenty to thirty yards that flattens or goes slightly uphill at the end.

2 Take the bike (without training wheels) and the kid to the spot.

3 Lower the seat so your child's feet can rest flat on the ground while seated. Put on her helmet and tuck in any loose clothing.

4 Position the bike halfway up the hill and hold it while your child sits in the saddle, feet on the ground. Let go of the bike.

5 When you are both ready, have her lift her feet off the ground about an inch and let her coast down the hill. Remind her that if she begins to lose her balance she can put her feet down to keep herself upright. Repeat this until she can coast without putting her feet down.

6 Next have her try it with her feet on level pedals.

7 After she's had a few successful runs, have her turn the pedals. Raise the seat so that when the leg on the downward pedal is extended it has a slight bend. When she is comfortable pedaling, let her coast from the top of the hill.

8 Do a few more runs of coasting and pedaling from the top of the incline. She can also incorporate some braking and turning at the bottom of the hill.

9 Next, move to an open and level spot, such as a field, a parking lot, or a cul-de-sac, and practice starting, stopping, and turning.

SUPER TIP

Attach pierced earrings or barrettes to a piece of fabric or ribbon to keep them organized.

—LAUREN, MOM OF ISABELLA

106

Paddle a Canoe

Each summer my dad took some of the kids and the canoe to a campsite on the edge of a river or lake. Which is why, the first two things my dad said when I asked him for tips on canoeing with kids were, "Make sure everyone is wearing a life jacket," and "Put the child at the front." Both have to do with safety, the first for obvious reasons. The second is not as obvious if you don't know that it's the person in the rear who's steering the canoe. Beginners should canoe on flat, still water, such as a lake. If your family enjoys paddling and intends to do it regularly, the best and safest way to be prepared is to get instructions. You can contact the American Canoe Association for information on lessons. In the meantime, to get a taste, here is how to paddle the basic forward stroke with two people.

1 First, you want the canoe to sit as close to level as possible. If anything, the rear (the stern) could sit slightly lower than the front (the bow), but never the reverse. If there is a large weight discrepancy between you and your child, you can even it out by placing your baggage (or weights) in the bow.

2 To paddle a canoe straight, two people should paddle in sync, on opposite sides of the canoe. Have your child paddle in front on whatever side is comfortable. She can change sides whenever she needs to. You should follow her lead and change sides as required to keep the canoe moving straight.

3 Grip the paddle correctly. Hold it with one hand on the top of the grip and the other on the shaft. Your hands should be roughly arm's length or shoulder-width apart.

4 The paddle enters the water on the side of the canoe opposite the hand holding the grip.

5 Reach forward and insert the blade of the paddle deep and straight into the water. It should enter ahead of your knees as far as you can comfortably reach. Keep the paddle blade perpendicular to the canoe and the shaft perpendicular to the water.

6 Pull the paddle straight toward you only as far as your knee, lift the blade straight out of the water, and insert it in the water ahead of you for the next stroke. Keeping your strokes short and even will help you maintain the correct form and keep the canoe moving smoothly.

7 Because you will be in the back you will hold and correct the course of the canoe. If you are paddling on the left and the canoe is going too far to the left, paddle on right side to straighten your course.

107

Tie a Few Good Knots

There are many knots and each has it's own purpose. The bowline is a loop fixed with a knot and is good for a rescue line. The sheet bend knot can be used to tie lengths of rope together and will hold if the ropes are of different widths. A good secure hitch knot is the round turn and two half hitches.

figure 1

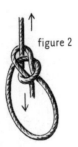
figure 2

THE BOWLINE KNOT

1 Hold the rope with one hand where the knot in the loop will be. Create a small loop there by bringing the end of the rope on top.

2 Thread the end through the loop and behind the long end, figure 1, then back down through the loop, figure 2.

3 Tighten.

THE SHEET BEND KNOT

1 First make a loop with the end of one rope.

2 Thread the end of another rope into the loop from underneath, then out of the loop and around the base.

3 Bring the rope back into the loop and thread it under itself and over the loop, figure 3. (For a square knot the end comes straight out and under the loop.)

4 Tighten.

figure 3

THE ROUND TURN & TWO HALF HITCHES KNOT

1 Loop the rope around a pole twice so both ends come out in the same direction.

2 Cross the leading end over the rope and back around through the loop you created, figure 4. Thread it over and back around through the next loop, figure 5.

3 Tighten.

figure 4

figure 5

108

Whistle Using Your Fingers

When Richard wanted to learn to whistle, I told him how to hold his lips and where to position his tongue when he blew out the air. The more he tried the more frustrated he became. I told him he had to be patient and keep trying. I read him A Whistle for Willie by Ezra Jack Keats, which was not too reassuring because, of course, Willie could whistle by the time the story was over. Richard persisted and soon enough he was whistling proudly.

The thing I really wanted to teach him, but couldn't because I didn't know how myself, was how to whistle loudly using two fingers. I can teach him now thanks to my neighbor Lisa. The first thing you need to know is that whistling doesn't come easily; it requires a lot of practice and perseverance. The goal is to use your fingers, tongue, lips, and teeth to force the air to flow through your mouth and out the space created by your fingers. Much of the practice will involve making slight adjustments to the position of your tongue, fingers, and lips.

1 Put the tips of your thumb and your forefinger (or middle finger or two pinkies; one of the elements you will be experimenting with) together, so the ends of the fingernails just about touch.

2 Wrap your lips over your teeth, and pull them into your mouth.

3 Roll the tip of your tongue back over on itself.

4 Put your fingers in your mouth roughly to a point between your knuckles and the first joint, with the tips of your fingers pointed slightly downward and pushing gently on the underside of your curled tongue. (This is the other arrangement you'll be fine-tuning as you practice.)

5 Create a tight seal with your fingers so the air you blow does not go out the sides but flows out the space created between your fingers and your lips.

6 Eventually, you will begin to make a quiet whistle. Keep practicing and you will begin to get a feel for exactly how to position all the key elements to produce the sound.

7 Resist the urge to blow too hard while you practice; you'll become dizzy from lack of breath, as I can attest.

Identify Poison Ivy

Leaves of three, let it be" is an expression used to help kids remember to beware of poison ivy. Although this is not all you need to know, if you heed it you'll likely avoid poison ivy. You may be avoiding harmless plants as well, but better safe than sorry. Following are additional characteristics that distinguish poison ivy.

1 Each set of three leaflets is considered a leaf. The middle of the three leaflets is on a longer stem and may be slightly larger than the outer two, which oppose each other.

2 The leaves alternate on the main stem.

3 The tips of the leaflets are generally pointed and the edges can be smooth or lobed, figure 1.

4 It can grow as a ground cover, a shrub, or a vine. In the fall the leaves turn a brilliant red and it later produces clusters of white berries.

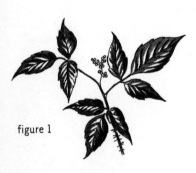

figure 1

110

Jump Rope

t's easy to take really basic things, such as jumping rope, for granted. But when your five-year-old wants to jump rope and can't get the hang of it, there are some tips that could help her master the skill with a little less frustration.

1 The first thing to know is that the right size jump rope should come up to your armpits at the ends when you stand on it in the middle and hold one end in each hand. Also, it shouldn't be too light or it won't turn well.

2 Start with the rope behind you, at your heels.

3 Keep your elbows close to your body and use as little arm movement as possible, turning the rope primarily with your wrists.

4 Jump on the balls of your feet, with your feet together and knees slightly bent, using small, soft jumps.

5 For beginners it might be easier to make two jumps per revolution. Then you can move on to one jump per revolution.

Build a Simple Snowman

Mommy, let's make a snowman!!!" It's a simple enough request for parents who have grown up in snowy climates. But if you haven't had much experience, here are a few tips. First you need the right conditions. If the air is too cold and dry the snow won't pack well and hold together when you form it into a ball. Second, keep old hats, gloves, mittens, and scarves, along with some chunks of coal or rocks, in a bag near your snow shovels. When it snows, your snowman kit will be handy.

1 Form three balls: big, bigger, and biggest. Roll each around in the snow and pack snow onto it as you go.

2 Finish rolling the biggest ball at the spot where you want the snowman to stand.

3 Finish the second ball close to the first ball so you don't have far to lift it.

4 Place the second ball on top of the first and the third ball, the smallest, on top of the second.

5 Pack some extra snow where the parts meet to make your snowman more stable.

6 If the snow isn't sticking and it's sunny, try rolling where the sun is shining. The snow may be wetter there and will stick better. If the snow still doesn't pack well, fill a garbage can with tightly packed snow and carefully dump it after a day or two. Carve the snow away to form the traditional three-ball shape.

7 Find some branches for arms, and be creative with decorations:

* Old leaves, fir tree branches, or pinecones sticking out of the snow can be hair.

* Go to your vegetable drawer. A carrot for the nose, yes, but how about a red pepper or radishes for the mouth or oranges as eyes?

* Give him a snow shovel or ski poles to hold.

* For a bit of fun, use sunglasses or ski goggles for eyes.

SUPER TIP

When you begin to throw out some of the crafts your child brought home from preschool (you will), save and recycle the googly eyes, pipe cleaners, and anything else that might be useful.

—MARY JO, MOM OF MICHAEL AND ANDREW

Skim Stones

As a child, my summer vacation each year was spent camping with my father and some of my siblings. We always camped on a lake or river so that we could keep a canoe in the water and use it at will. When we weren't hiking or canoeing, my sisters and I could be found at the water's edge skimming stones. It's not just the act of skimming the stone that I remember. For me, the search for the perfect stone was part of the pleasure.

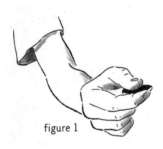

figure 1

1 Look for a stone that is roughly the size of your palm; it should be as smooth and as flat as you can find. Some sources say a circular stone is best, but according to stone skimming champion, Jerdone Coleman-McGee, a triangular shape is best. When you're at the water's edge you can see what works best for you.

2 Speaking of water, smooth and still is better than wavy or flowing water.

3 The grip and the throw are also important factors. Hold

the stone around its outer edge with your forefinger, allowing it to rest on your middle finger with your thumb on top, figure 1.

4 Face the water, bring your throwing arm back, and lean back and sideways for a sidearm throw, figure 2. When your arm comes forward and is fully extended, release the stone with a strong snap of your wrist; this gives it spin. The speed of the throw is important, but the spin is more important. The spin stabilizes the stone, enabling it to bounce over rather than fall into the water. The stone should have speed and spin and be nearly parallel to the water when it makes contact.

figure 2

Hit a Baseball

Even kids who don't want to be on a baseball team, need to know how to hit the ball well enough to enjoy pick-up games and gym class. I got these tips from my brother, Tom, who coached his son and daughter, both of whom were formidable hitters for their little league teams.

* Buy lots of standard-size Wiffle balls, some of the big ones to start with, and a fat plastic bat. Begin pitching; repetition is the key.

* A good way to begin, according to my friend Donna's brother, is to ask your child to show you his swing. See where he is swinging and pitch to that spot.

* Teach them how to stand: A righty swinger should stand with her left foot forward and just the toe touching the ground. This will teach her to shift her weight from the back to the front as she brings her foot to the ground when swinging at the ball. Also, she should stand perpendicular to you and just turn her head to face you. The bat should be over her shoulder and her elbows should be up (but at the same time, her shoulders should be relaxed).

✳ Tell him to keep his eye on the ball. That may seem obvious to you, but he will look at your face, not at the ball.

✳ As she improves, you can pitch Wiffle golf balls. Then when you go back to the standard Wiffle ball it will seem like an easier target.

✳ Another drill as he gets better is to stand behind him and throw the ball over his head so it comes down in the box. This will teach him to concentrate and to respond quickly.

✳ The key is to give her confidence. Any kid enjoys baseball once she has gotten a good piece of the ball.

SUPER TIP

To pass time while doing adult-type waiting, such as in a doctor's office: Take turns tracing shapes, numbers, or letters on one another's back and guessing what you made. Also take turns finding things that rhyme.

—LINDA, MOM OF CONNOR AND ELENA

Make Bubble Prints

My kids saw this on "Teletubbies" and insisted on trying it themselves. We've done it quite a few times, and they love the results. Richard likes to do this on circles and pretend he is making planets, so we use paper plates. It gets messy, so put down newspaper before you start.

WHAT YOU'LL NEED

small bowls or containers
liquid dish detergent
tempera paints
straws
paper or paper plates

1 In a shallow container with a wide, open top (some Tupperware containers are perfect), combine ¼ cup of the liquid dish detergent with one color of tempera paint until the color is strong. Mix other colors in separate bowls.

2 Put the straw into the bowl and blow into the mixture until the bubbles begin to overflow (be careful not to ingest any of the mixture).

3 Place a piece of paper or a paper plate onto the mountain of bubbles. Take it off and let it dry, or place it on a different color. Enjoy the patterns the colored bubbles leave behind.

115

Make a Purse

My daughter Anita can't have enough purses. She enjoys them all equally, from her Barbie purse to grandma's hand-me-down purse. My personal fave is the one I made for her from a pair of old blue jeans and a piece of ribbon.

WHAT YOU'LL NEED
an old pair of blue jeans or other pants
needle and thread
a piece of ribbon or rope
some Velcro
materials to use as decoration (optional)

1 Cut one leg about 7 inches from the bottom. Turn it inside out.

2 Sew the cut end together in a straight line across. Turn it right side out.

3 Sew a nice piece of ribbon or rope from seam to seam for the shoulder strap.

4 Stick Velcro inside at the top center for the clasp.

5 Decorate the outside as desired with fabric paint, glitter glue, patches of felt or fabric, buttons, pom-poms, or embroidery.

Make Play Figures

Kids often want to play with toy figures recreating scenes, whether it be something they've seen on television or in the movies or something they've imagined. These homemade substitutes actually appeal to kids, and helps them rely even more on their own imagination.

WHAT YOU'LL NEED
toilet paper tubes
crayons or markers
scissors
construction paper, fabric, or felt
glue

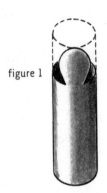

figure 1

1 Hold the tube on end and draw a circle a little bigger than a quarter at the top. This will be the head of the figure. Then draw a line around the tube at the base of the circle.

2 With scissors, cut along the line, don't cut off the circle, figure 1.

3 Use construction paper, fabric, or felt to make clothes, hair, a mask, and a cape. Make the clothes so they wrap around the tube.

4 Draw on the face and glue on the hair and clothes.

5 For legs, draw a line down the center on the bottom half.

Pumpkin Seed Jewelery

When you are preparing to carve your pumpkin and you've emptied the guts, save the seeds. Soak them in water to separate them from the pulp. Then lay them out to dry on a paper towel. Don't allow them to become brittle or they'll crack when you try to use them.

WHAT YOU'LL NEED

pumkin seeds
needle and thread or elastic thread
food coloring

* String them together by sticking a threaded needle through the flat side one at a time. If you use thread, make a long enough strand to go over your child's head. For a bracelet or a shorter necklace you should use elasticized thread. Tie the ends together in a knot.

* You can also try threading the seeds from end to end, rather than back to back, so they lie flat.

* If you want to have some color, add food coloring to the water while the seeds are soaking. Soak them in a variety of colors so you can create patterns when you thread them.

Make Frames (from paper plates)

At my pediatrician's office there are lots of pictures hanging on the cabinet doors. The pictures are framed in the center of white plastic and paper plates. The plates make a surprisingly nice display for something so simple. Think of the fun children can have coloring and decorating the borders. Paper plates work well for coloring; plastic works well for gluing on beads and other objects.

WHAT YOU'LL NEED

photos that can be cut
and glued
scissors
pencil
paper or plastic plates
crayons, markers, or paints
glue
beads, buttons, pom-poms,
glitter, stickers, etc.

1 If you want to, cut the picture into another size or shape. With a pencil, trace the shape of the picture in the center of the plate.

2 Use crayons, markers, or paints to color and/or decorate around the traced shape. Glue on beads and other items.

3 Glue the photo in the traced shape.

119

Make a Flip Book

Being able to make a flip book will really make your kids feel like you are a superhero, because there is an element of magic in the way these work.

WHAT YOU'LL NEED

10 business or index cards
a large clip
(or a Post-it pad)
a pencil, crayons or markers
stamps or stickers (optional)

1 First come up with a simple scene, such as a train riding on train rails, a butterfly flying around a flower, or the sun setting behind a mountain.

2 Attach ten or so business or index cards together with a big clip (a Post-it notepad also works great). On the blank side of each page, draw the stationary elements (the train rails, the flower, or the mountain) in pencil.

3 Starting on the last page, draw the beginning of the moving "story." Draw close enough to the bottom edge of the pad so the action will be visible. Change the position of the moving elements slightly on each successive page until you have drawn the final scene.

4 Test it out by flipping the pages. Make any adjustments that are needed. You can color it in if you want.

5 Small children can use stamps or stickers so they don't have to try to draw the same thing again and again.

120

Make Sock Puppets

Does anyone darn socks anymore? I don't think so. It's better to keep your old socks in your craft drawer and pull them out when you need an emergency sock puppet. These can be as plain or as complicated as you want. You can simply put it over your hand and draw a face on it or you can sew on eyes, a tongue, clothes, hair, a hat...

WHAT YOU'LL NEED
adult-size sock
needle and thread or glue
fabric or felt
markers or fabric paint
buttons or sequins
pom-poms
yarn
big serving spoon or paper towel tube

✱ Put the sock over your hand. Experiment with the shape of your hand and the position of the sock. You'll be surprised at how expressive it can be.

✱ Decide what your puppet is going to be based on the color of the sock. Gray is good for an elephant; green is a natural for a frog. A white one is good if you just want to make a face.

✱ To make an elephant, pull the toe out a couple of inches, twist it around, and sew it into position to form the trunk, then sew on felt or fabric to make big ears.

✱ To make a frog, place the heel of the sock along the back of your wrist. Create a mouth by pulling the toe out a bit and then stuffing it between your fingers and your thumb. You can draw or sew on a tongue and eyes.

✳ To make a face, put your hand in the sock, fold your fingers over, and draw or sew a face on top of your fingers. Use buttons or sequins for eyes; a pom-pom for a nose; yarn for hair; and fabric and felt for the ears, mouth, tongue, a hat, and clothes. Tie fabric around your wrist for a collar or cape.

✳ Put your fingers in the toe and your thumb in the heel to create a big wide mouth. Bunch little corners of the sock and sew them in place for ears.

✳ When you are ready to sew or glue on the items, put the sock over a big serving spoon or a paper towel tube to hold it in place and give you two free hands.

SUPER TIP

You may have heard of "painting" the driveway with water and paintbrushes. Take it a step further. "Clean" the driveway with buckets of water, mops and brooms.

—LYNN, MOM OF JACKIE, STEVEN AND NICHOLAS

121

CRAFT

Make Butterfly Wings

All kids like to pretend to fly. You can make simple butterfly wings with a paper grocery bag.

WHAT YOU'LL NEED

a paper grocery bag
scissors
crayons or markers
a stapler

1 Cut the bag and open it so it is a large flat sheet.

2 Draw the shape of wings on the bag so they are as wide as your child's outstretched arms. You can refer to a book if you need to know what shape to make the wings, or use the diagram as reference for a wing shape.

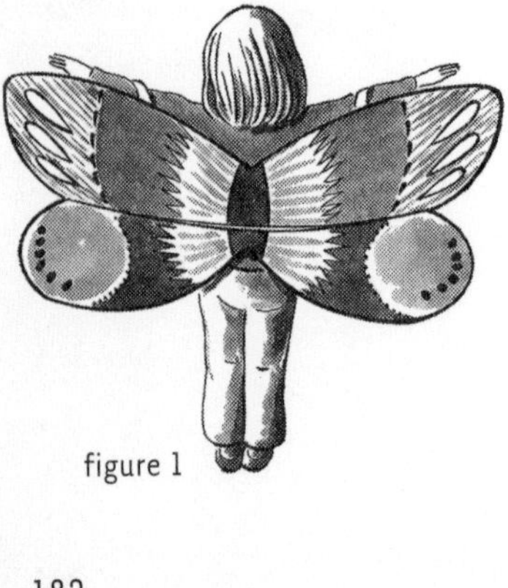

figure 1

3 Have your child color the wings.

4 Staple a 1½-inch-wide strip of paper to each wing to hold them in place on the arms. Have your child lie on top of the bag with her arms outstretched, then position each strap over each forearm.

5 Slip an arm into each strap so the wings span across her back, figure 1.

6 If you want the wings to last longer, use felt or fabric instead of paper and sew on the straps.

CRAFT | ✺

Cardboard Box Buildings

When Richard was in kindergarten, one of the moms, an architect, did this as a project with the kids (another good example of learning from a superhero mom). I thought it was a really fun way to teach them about relative shapes and sizes.

WHAT YOU'LL NEED
a variety of cardboard boxes
construction paper or paint
glue

1 Save cardboard boxes and tubes in a variety of shapes and sizes. Wrap ones that have a lot printed on them with white paper or construction paper. Or paint them a solid color.

2 Help your child assemble an arrangement into a build-

ing or a castle. A roof can be made by folding a flat piece of cardboard in half and placing it on top.

3 Glue the structure together. Make windows and doors from construction paper and glue them on, or draw directly onto the building.

4 Make a bunch of buildings to create a town for car and train sets.

123

Make a Snow Globe

Figuring out what to put inside the globe should be easy if your kids have little plastic toys, such as dinosaurs, Legos, or ballerinas, from goody bags. Plastic cake toppers and character tops from bubble bath bottles work, too. Just make sure you have a jar that will fit the object.

Obviously, the fun of snow globes is watching the "snow" swirl around the object. The liquid you use to fill the jar is what determines how fast or how slow the snow will sink. You can use baby oil for a good slow effect. I prefer to add some dishwashing liquid to water.

WHAT YOU'LL NEED
a small jar
an object for inside
hot glue or superglue
liquid dish detergent
glitter
tape

1 Wash the jar and the top thoroughly, removing the label.

2 Make sure you'll be able to screw the lid onto the jar when the object is glued onto the lid.

3 Glue the object onto the lid with either a hot glue gun or

Superglue, and allow it to dry thoroughly.

4 Fill the jar with water and squeeze in some liquid dish detergent. Leave a little space at the top because the object will displace some of the water. Add glitter for snow.

5 Screw the top on tightly. You can tape or glue the edge of the top for added protection.

6 If you like, you can paint or decorate the jar top, which is the base of your snow globe.

Make A Telescope

When I made this for the first time I was lucky enough to have two toilet paper tubes that were not exactly the same size. One tube could slip in and out of the other. That phenomenon has not occurred again, so I just use paper towel tubes, which are almost as much fun.

WHAT YOU'LL NEED
a paper towel tube (or two toilet paper tubes)
construction paper
crayons or markers
stickers, yarn

1 Cover the paper towel tube with construction paper. Color or decorate it with crayons, markers, stickers, yarn, or whatever you have on hand.

2 If you do happen to have toilet paper tubes that slip inside one another, cover the larger, outside one with construction paper and any three-dimensional decorations, and color the inner one with markers and crayon.

125

Make Dresses for Barbie

One my friends has an overabundance of pillowcases in her house, so she doesn't mind ripping them up to make Barbie dresses, but you could also use pieces of felt or any old clothes for this. And don't worry if you can't sew; the point of these clothes is that they should look homemade and that your kids can help you with them. (Remember, you are doing this with a young child, and this isn't a sewing lesson. Your only goal here is to make something quick for Barbie, not an heirloom.)

WHAT YOU'LL NEED
pillowcases, old clothes, felt, or scrap material
pen or pencil
scissors
cardboard (optional)
safety pins
needle and thread
ribbon and sequins (optional)

1 Give your children a choice of fabrics and ask what type of clothes they want to make.

2 Turn the fabric inside out, lay Barbie on top, and have them roughly trace the doll's body onto the cloth with a pen. By "roughly" I mean they can go as much as a ½ inch outside of Barbie's body, which will accommodate loose sewing.

3 With scissors, cut out clothes from the fabric. Alternatively, you can make a cardboard "pattern" and use that to cut out the material. Pin the back and front pieces together.

4 Draw a straight line about ¼ to ½ inch away from the edge of the material. This is the line they will follow when they sew. They can either sew right on the line, or, if they're really young, you can have them loop over the edges.

5 Finish the sewing and then turn the clothes inside out and slip them over Barbie's head and legs.

6 Feel free to use ribbons to make belts or to sew sequins on the clothes.

By the way, there are real patterns out there for Barbie and other doll clothes, and I applaud anyone who can make those.

Make a Sun Catcher

We used wax paper and an iron to make these when I was a kid, but contact paper works well, too. Especially if your iron is buried in the back of a closet. You can use pressed flowers and leaves (see page 23) or colored tissue paper cut or torn into shapes. I recall cutting thin strips of black construction paper and using them to separate one color from the other so it would look like stained glass. You can also use yarn to separate the colors or to create a design.

WHAT YOU'LL NEED

wax paper or contact paper
tissue paper, pressed flowers, yarn
an iron and a pillow case or glue
some thread

WITH WAX PAPER

Create your design by placing the tissue paper, pressed flower, or yarn onto a sheet of wax paper. Put another piece of wax paper over the design. Carefully iron it under a pil-lowcase without disturbing the design. Smaller children could just glue the materials directly onto the wax paper). Punch a hole in the wax paper and hang it in a window with some thread.

WITH CONTACT PAPER

Place the elements of the design onto the sticky side of some contact paper, then cover with another piece of contact paper. Punch a hole in it and hang.

Make a Chinese Lantern

This is a very simple thing to make with construction paper and it's great to use as a party decoration.

WHAT YOU'LL NEED
construction paper
scissors
a stapler or clear tape

1 Fold a piece of paper in half lengthwise.

2 Cut 3-inch slits along the length of the folded side of the paper, ½ to 1 inch apart.

3 Unfold the paper. Curl the paper around and tape or staple the short ends together. The fold should be facing out, creating a convex shape.

4 Cut a 1-inch-wide strip of construction paper and staple it onto the top of the lantern to make a handle, figure 1.

figure 1

Make a Puzzle

K ids get a kick out of creating puzzles from pictures they choose because it seems like such a personal treat. Use a picture your child has drawn, a family photograph, or a picture from a magazine. This is an especially good gift for a child to give an older relative.

WHAT YOU'LL NEED
a photograph or picture
glue
a pencil
a craft knife
cardboard

1 Have your child glue the picture to a piece of stiff, thick cardboard.

2 When it has dried, trim off any excess cardboard around the edges.

3 Turn it over and draw the lines for the puzzle on the back. Cut along the lines with a craft knife to make the pieces.

Flowers from Egg Cartons

There a lot of crafty ways to make flowers, but some are more amusing and imaginative than others. For some reason, this one brings back very fond memories for me. It is a collage using the cups from cardboard egg cartons as flowers.

WHAT YOU'LL NEED
a cardboard egg carton
a piece of cardboard
construction paper
scissors
glue
pom-poms or buttons
crayons, markers or paint

1 With green construction paper, draw and cut out leaves and stems; glue onto cardboard.

2 Cut out the cup sections of an egg carton to make flowers:

DAISY Cut the corners of the cup down from the top, flatten the sections, glue a button in the center.

DAFFODIL Glue an uncut cup on top of a flattened one.

DAHLIA Cut a couple of sections with many pointed petals. Flatten them, glue them on top of each other, and add a pom-pom center.

TULIP Cut rounded edges along the top.

ROSE Cut a few sections with rounded edges at different heights and glue them inside one another.

3 Color or paint the flowers.

4 Glue them in position on the ends of the stems so the petals to rise off the paper.

130

Make Pom-Pom Animals

One of my grandmother's friends made little animals from pom-poms when I was a child. I always felt they were the sweetest little creatures. With just a few materials you can make mice, birds, kittens, frogs, lions...

WHAT YOU'LL NEED
yarn
cardboard
scissors
glue
googly eyes, pipe cleaners, felt

figure 1

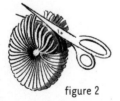

figure 2

1 First, make the pom-poms. Cut out two circles of cardboard roughly 1 inch more in diameter than the desired size of the pom-pom.

2 Cut a 1-inch hole in the center of the cardboard circles so they look like doughnuts.

3 Put the two pieces of cardboard together and wrap yarn through the hole and around the "doughnuts", figure 1, until they are completely wrapped with yarn.

4 With scissors, cut the yarn between the two pieces of cardboard, figure 2.

figure 3

5 Use a longer piece of yarn to tie around the center of the yarn, between the cardboard circles, figure 3. Remove the cardboard. Trim the pom-pom to make it even.

6 To make animals, cut small ears, beaks, tails, and feet from felt and glue them on along with some googly eyes. Use pipe cleaners for whiskers or limbs.

Make a Sword

I f you have a boy, sooner or later he will want a sword, whether it's because he wants to be a knight for Halloween or because he wants to have a sword fight with his friend after watching *The Princess Bride.* Either way, boys see weapons in everyday objects, so it will help if you can see weapons in everyday objects, too. Swords are quick and easy to make, and he'll have hours of fun with it. While you're at it, you might as well make two so he can fence with his pal.

WHAT YOU'LL NEED

cardboard wrapping paper
tube
scissors
Scotch tape
aluminum foil
black electrical tape
dinner-sized paper plate

1 Flatten the tube and cut one end into a point with the scissors. Tape it closed with Scotch tape.

2 Wrap the tube with foil, and then tape the seams with Scotch tape.

3 Wrap black tape up to about 10 inches on the end of the tube that isn't pointed.

4 Fold the paper plate in half and cut out the center, leaving just the frame.

5 Keeping the paper plate folded, slip it over the unpointed end of the sword to form the handle guard.

6 Tape the paper plate in place with the black tape.

7 Wrap the rest of the paper plate with the black tape.

132

Make Family Puppets

Kids often like to hear stories about themselves. To really get their attention, help them make puppets of each person in the family. Then you can tell the story in a puppet show or they can tell their own story with familiar characters.

WHAT YOU'LL NEED
family photographs
scissors
glue
scissors
a straw or Popsicle stick
felt, fabric or construcion paper

Cut out snapshots of people in your family and glue them to a straw or a Popsicle stick. You can cut out the entire figure, or you can cut out just the head and add the bodies using felt, fabric, or construction paper.

SUPER TIP

Keep stickers in your diaper bag to keep baby busy (trying to pull them up). Always watch and make sure they don't put the stickers in their mouth.

—KATE, MOM OF SAM

133

Make Paper Dolls (and clothes)

These don't have to only be for girls. Boys can have action figure or hero dolls, such as knights and pirates. Or make the dolls look like your family by gluing your photos onto their heads.

WHAT YOU'LL NEED
pencil
card stock
tracing paper (optional)
scissors
crayons or markers
construction paper or wrapping paper scraps
clothing circulars
or magazines

1 With pencil, draw the doll on card stock.

2 Your child will probably be happy with your drawing. But if you aren't, you can trace figures from children's books or coloring books, which often

have simple line figures. Find a figure whose clothing does not make it too difficult to trace the outline of the body.

3 Trace the outline of the figure onto tracing paper. Include the details of the face and hair, but not the clothing.

4 Place the tracing paper on card stock, then draw over the tracing, pressing hard enough to leave an impression on the card stock. Include the face details.

5 Draw over the impression, and use scissors to cut out the doll.

6 Draw undergarments on the figure. Color them in or have your child color them.

7 To make the clothing, simply place the doll over construction paper and trace around her. You can make pants, shirts, skirts, dresses, shoes, hats, handbags, toys, and more. Use white or colored paper and add your own patterns, or use patterned paper such as wrapping paper scraps.

8 If you look through clothing circulars or magazines you can find things that "fit" your doll. Or cut clothing from the fabrics pictured. If you want to be able to secure the clothing to the doll, draw tabs before you cut out the clothing. Or your child can simply mix and match the clothing, laying it over the doll.

9 If you want the doll to stand you need to make a base. Before you cut out the figure, draw a half circle from the doll's calves to the edge of her feet, with the straight edge perpendicular to the figure. When you cut out the doll, cut around the semicircle, not her feet. Cut a slit in the bottom at the center. Cut a freestanding half circle the same size as the first. Cut a slit in the center at the top. Slide it into the slit at the base of the doll.

10 If tracing your own doll is too complicated, find a figure in an ad for underclothes or bathing suits. Glue the figure onto card stock, cut it out, and dress it.

11 Another option is to go online, where you can print out templates of paper dolls and clothing directly onto card stock.

134

Make a Pinwheel

f you have a budding scientist who wants to learn a little about wind and optical illusions, you can create a few of these. Experiment with different papers and see which one works best. Try different colors and patterns and observe the various optical effects they create. This is not a project for toddlers, though, because it involves a pin.

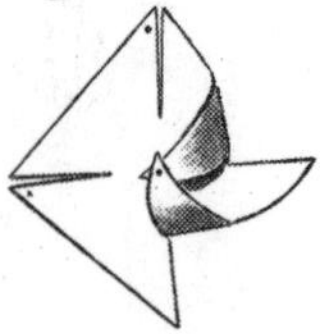

WHAT YOU'LL NEED
scissors
ruler
sturdy sheet of paper
pen or pencil
sewing pin with a head
paper clip
unsharpened pencil with an
unused eraser
bead (optional)

figure 1

figure 2

1 Cut a 5-inch square from the sheet of paper. Draw diagonal lines on the paper from corner to corner.

2 Mark 1 inch out from the center on each line. Cut along the lines from the corner to the point you marked, figure 1.

3 With the pin, make a hole in the center and in one corner of each triangle. Make the hole in the same spot on each corner.

4 Enlarge the holes slightly with a paper clip to allow your pinwheel to move freely.

5 Thread the pin through the back of each corner hole, then through the center hole, figure 2. Press the pin into the eraser of the pencil. If you are using a small bead, thread it on first, figure 3. This will separate the paper from the pencil, allowing the pinwheel to move more freely.

6 Allow the front (the corners) to come forward to the head of the pin. The gap between the front and back will allow the pinwheel to catch the wind.

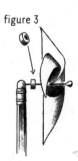

figure 3

135

Make Paper Chains

This was something we did as children around Christmas. I always thought the purpose was to decorate the house. But recently my mom told me we did it because it kept us busy while she was trying to get her housework finished. Your kids can do it any time of year, whenever you need time to get something accomplished.

WHAT YOU'LL NEED
scissors
construction paper in different colors
glue stick, Scotch tape, or stapler

1 If your children are old enough, have them cut construction paper widthwise into 1-inch strips. If they're too young, you do the cutting.

2 Form a loop and glue the ends together to hold it in place. You can also use Scotch tape or a stapler if the kids are old enough. Take another strip and feed it through the first. Make a loop, linking it to the first loop. Secure it with glue and continue along until you have a chain.

3 Use different colors to make a repeating pattern, if desired.

Make Binoculars

This is the perfect supermom project, because it requires something that you would otherwise throw out and will become something that your kids think is supercool. Also, they will do most of the work, which makes it supercool for you.

WHAT YOU'LL NEED
two toilet paper tubes
glue
construction paper
markers or crayons, sequins,
yarn

1 Wrap construction paper around two toilet paper tubes. Glue the two tubes together side by side.

2 When they are dry, let your child color and decorate them with crayons, markers, yarn, or sequins.

3 Put a hole on each side and attach some yarn so she can wear them around her neck.

137

Make a Rocket (from a paper towel tube)

figure 1

One evening we were watching a movie about some kids from the golden age of space travel who teamed up to build a working rocket ship. Richard wanted to have his own to play with that night. Thankfully, after a discussion about safety, he was satisfied with one that didn't actually involve explosives.

WHAT YOU'LL NEED

scissors
paper towel tube
markers
cardboard shirt box
tape
2 toilet paper tubes

1 Cut four equally spaced 2-inch slits in the bottom of the paper towel tube.

2 Decorate the tube with the markers.

3 Using a piece of the cardboard shirt box and tape, create a cone shape with an open end that matches the diameter of the paper towel tube. Tape the cone to the top of the tube.

4 Cut the two toilet paper tubes along the seam that runs around them, and uncurl them.

5 Cut off the triangular ends so the cut edge is about 2½ inches long. Flatten them as much as you can.

6 Slide the triangle shapes into the slits you cut at the base of the tube. Tape them in place, figure 1.

SUPER TIP

Kids will be happy to play with anything of yours that doesn't work anymore, such as a camera, a keyboard, or a phone. Just make sure they can't plug it into anything and that there is nothing sharp involved.

—BETH, MOM OF TIMOTHY

CRAFT ✂

Make a Photo Album

When Anita was going through separation anxiety at around age two, I filled a small, plush covered photo album with pictures. She brought it to daycare and could look at us whenever she wanted. After that passed, she got a lot of pleasure from having her own photo album. When John wanted one, I made one with sandwich bags and two potholders.

WHAT YOU'LL NEED
six 4 x 6 snapshots
3 plastic sandwich bags
2 potholders
needle and thread

1 Stack the bags between the potholders with the openings on the right so you'll be able to change the pictures.

2 Sew the left edge together.

3 Place two photos back to back in each of the bags.

SUPER TIP

Keep your baby occupied with a box of tissues (they can pull them out), a calculator (they can press the buttons), or a roll of Scotch tape (they can unravel the tape).

—EILEEN, MOM OF ROBERT

Make a Caterpillar

Cardboard egg cartons (like toilet paper tubes) are extremely valuable when you have children. There are so many things you can make from them. The things you can do with the carton gives you good reasons to eat eggs. One of my favorite things to make is a caterpillar.

WHAT YOU'LL NEED
scissors
egg carton
construction paper
10 twist ties
pipe cleaner
markers
glue

1 With scissors, cut the egg carton in half lengthwise.

2 Cut dime-size circles from the construction paper.

3 Cut the pipe cleaner in half and curl one end of each half into spirals to make antennae.

4 To make legs, accordion-bend the twist ties so there are three equal segments and one shorter segment, which will hold it in place on the egg carton.

5 With markers, draw a face on the end segment of the carton. With the point of the scissors, poke holes on top for the antennae.

6 Make ten slits, one on each side of the other five segments, for the legs.

7 Glue the circles on the carton to decorate the caterpillar's body.

8 Put glue on the ends of the antennae and the tabs of the legs and insert them in the correct places.

140

Make Tissue Paper Flowers

I used to love making tissue paper flowers when I was a child. I always made them accordion-style, which are the directions that follow, though I have since seen some variations. All you need is tissue paper and pipe cleaners. Make a bunch for a vase or twist some together for a crown.

figure 1

figure 2

figure 3

WHAT YOU'LL NEED

tissue paper
scissors
pipe cleaners
markers or watercolor paint
(optional)

1 Start with four to six pieces of tissue paper (the bigger the paper, the bigger the flower). You can layer different colors or use all one color. Or, use white paper and color it later.

2 Stack the papers evenly, then fold accordion-style, figure 1. Use ¾- to 1-inch folds for a medium-size flower, a bigger fold for big flowers, and a smaller fold for small flowers. You'll end up with a long strip.

3 You can cut each end of the folded strip. A rounded cut will give you rounded petals, and a pointed cut will give you pointed petals. If you want straight-edged petals, don't cut the ends.

4 Wrap the end of a pipe cleaner tightly around the center of the strip, figure 2.

5 Open the folds and carefully separate one layer of tissue paper at a time, figure 3.

6 If you want, run the tip of magic markers over the layers for a nice effect, or brush the edges with water color paint.

7 You can also use coffee filters. Stack a few together, then loop the end of a pipe cleaner through the middle and tighten. These can be colored beforehand with markers or watercolors.

8 To make a crown, simply twist the pipe cleaners around one another into a ring with the flowers facing out.

Make Button Bracelets

I n the age of Velcro and zippers, buttons—especially beautiful ones—
are hard to come by. So if you are lucky enough to have found a bunch
at a yard sale or inherited some from your grandmother, hang on to them.
They are like little treasures and useful for decorating all sorts of things.
(Never let small children play with buttons; they are a choking hazard.)

WHAT YOU'LL NEED
elastic string
buttons

1 Create a loop by threading the elastic through one hole on a button and tying a knot. You could string the buttons back to back, in a pattern, or randomly.

2 If you have some buttons with pretty faces that you want to show off, thread the buttons one at a time, through the back and down through the front, so they'll lie flat on the wrist.

3 You want to have the buttons tightly spaced so when the bracelet is tied they don't slide away from one another and expose the elastic.

4 To finish, thread the elastic through the empty hole on the first button, loop the thread around the button, and tie a knot.

Paper Bag Puppets

Paper bag puppets are an easy, fun thing to keep the kids occupied while you have your much-needed cup of coffee. And when you need a king for the puppet show, a paper bag is a quick understudy. All you need is your imagination.

WHAT YOU'LL NEED
brown paper sandwich bags
markers
glue
scissors
crayons
construction paper

Use the construction paper to create different puppets: big ears and whiskers for a rabbit, small pointy ears and whiskers for a cat, accordion arms and a crown for a king, big eyes and a tongue for a frog, a yellow or orange mane for a lion ... you get the idea.

SUPER TIP

When it snows, make some miniature snowmen and keep them in the freezer to look at after the snow has melted.

—CAROLYN, MOM OF HUGO AND CELESTE

143

CRAFT

Make a Sailboat

To satisfy your child's fascination with things that float requires knowledge of how to make at least one boat that will stay above water for more than just a few seconds. I especially like the one Richard made from a milk carton in his kindergarten class.

WHAT YOU'LL NEED

a pint or ½ pint size waxy cardboard milk container
a piece of paper
a popsicle stick or a straw
a small amount of clay

figure 1

1 Cut the container from the top, along the sides and bottom, 1 inch from the closed end, figure 1.

figure 2

2 Make a paper triangle for the sail. Attach it to the Popsicle stick or a straw 2 inches from the end. It can extend beyond the top.

3 Place clay into the center of the boat to hold the sail, figure 2.

144

Make a Paper Fan

These are a great first craft for toddlers. And if you make them on a hot day everyone will enjoy using them which will make your child feel extra special.

WHAT YOU'LL NEED

paper
crayons or markers

1 Fold an 8.5 x 11-inch sheet of paper accordion-style in about 1-inch increments. You might need to start the process with the first fold so they can use that line as a template.

2 Have your child decorate it with crayons and markers.

3 Fold one end up to form a handle. Open it up and cool off!

SUPER TIP

Use an old salad spinner (one that you find at a garage sale is perfect, since these can be expensive when they are new) to make spin art rather than buying a spin art kit.

—CHERY, MOM OF SPENCER

145

Make Face Paint

Occasionally, one of my kids asks me to paint his or her face. Usually, it's after we've been to a fair where a face-painting booth is offered, but the line was too long, and our patience too short. Face paint isn't always readily available, I've even used watercolor paint. But there's a better solution and it's a simple recipe.

WHAT YOU'LL NEED

1 teaspoon cornstarch
½ teaspoon cold cream
½ teaspoon water
food coloring

1 In a small bowl, combine the cornstarch and cold cream. Once smooth, add the water.

2 When that's blended, add the food coloring to make the desired color.

3 Apply with a brush or your fingers. Wash with soap and water.

SUPER TIP

Buy craft kits and supplies—such as popsicle sticks, beads, and sewing notions, when you see them on sale, and have them available for a rainy day.

—JENNIFER, MOM OF MAX AND SAM

Make a Pinata

Richard asked to do this many times before I finally broke down and agreed. I guess I was afraid of the mess (rightfully so) and the knowledge that his younger siblings would want to get in on the action as well (right again). But even my mom allowed us to do papier-mâché, Infact, I remember making papier-mâché eggs at Easter. If she could manage it with her eight kids, certainly I can swing it with just three.

WHAT YOU'LL NEED
balloon
small bowl
newspaper torn into strips
roughly 1 to 2 inches wide
and 6 inches long
papier-mâché paste
or liquid starch
tape
string or yarn
paint or tissue or crepe paper
scissors
glue
candy
paper towel tube (optional)
pipe cleaner (optional)
large paper or plastic cup
(optional)

If you are using paste rather than liquid starch, do that first.

PASTE
4 cups water (2 cold, 2 hot)
½ cup flour
2 tablespoons sugar

1 Bring 2 cups of water to a boil on the stovetop.

2 Combine the 2 cups of cold water and the flour and mix until it is smooth and lump-free. Add the smooth flour mixture to the boiling water.

3 Allow the mixture to come to a boil again. Remove it from the heat and mix in the sugar.

4 Once cooled, it's ready to use. (The paste could be saved in the refrigerator, but it spoils quickly, so it's better to make just what you need.)

PIÑATA

1 Inflate the balloon. Rest your balloon on the bowl so it doesn't roll away.

2 Dip the newspaper into the paste one strip at a time. Remove excess paste by pulling the strip between two fingers.

3 Cover the balloon completely with newspaper strips, leave the area around the knot uncovered. This is where you will remove the balloon and put in the candy. Let it dry.

4 Tape a length of string around the balloon to hang the piñata. Arrange the string so the balloon will hang with the knotted end at the top.

5 Do a second layer of newspaper, over the string, in the opposite direction from the first. Let it dry.

6 Do a third layer in yet another direction. Let it dry thoroughly.

7 Puncture the balloon with a pin and remove it.

8 You can paint the piñata or decorate it by cutting and gluing on the tissue or crepe paper. Tissue paper creates a flat pattern; crepe paper strips glued on in small loops or cut like strips of grass and layered make a more textural, three-dimensional pattern.

9 When the inside is dry, fill it with candy. You can glue some tissue paper over the hole.

VARIATIONS

With additional supplies and steps you can make a pig, a hot air balloon or dinosaur eggs. These steps should be done after the second layer has dried and then covered over with the third layer of papier-mâché.

figure 1

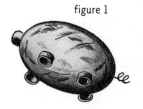

❋ Cut a paper towel tube into 1-inch sections and tape in place as the legs and snout of a pig, figure 1.

❋ Cut the paper cup in half. Tape the top of the cup to the bottom of the balloon, figure 2.

figure 2

❋ When the third layer is dry: glue a pipe cleaner in place as the tail of the pig, and attach the bottom of the cup to the top with some string for the basket of the hot air balloon.

❋ Use smaller balloons to start and decorate them to make colorful dinosaur eggs.

Make Your Own Play-Doh

I t's a little scary to think that there's little difference between Play-Doh and bread, but as you'll see, it's true. This is a great project to make with your kids not on a rainy day, as you might expect, but outside, as it's messy and you really won't want to end up with it on your floor (especially if there is a carpet underneath your feet).

WHAT YOU'LL NEED

4 cups flour
2 cups salt
2 cups water
4 tablespoons cream of tartar
2 tablespoons vegetable oil
food coloring (optional)

1 Mix all the ingredients in a big bowl.

2 If you want to add food coloring, do so just after it's all mixed together. Since this recipe makes about 6 cups of clay, you can divide up the mixture and make different color balls.

3 And, might I suggest having plastic utensils, as well as some big kitchen tools, such as a potato masher, on hand for the kids to use?

Make Your Own Silly Putty

Unlike home made Play-Doh, homemade Silly Putty does at least contain some nonedible ingredients (so you won't mistake it for your favorite bread recipe). It is also messy, so this is recommended as a nice outside day project.

WHAT YOU'LL NEED
½ cup white glue
½ cup liquid starch
food coloring (optional)
scented oil, such as peppermint (optional)

In a bowl, slowly mix the ingredients with your hands until it comes together. It will be really sticky. If it's not, add more glue.

SUPER TIP

*Use your kids' drawings and paintings for thank-you notes,
cards, letterhead, or wrapping paper.*

—PATTI, MOM OF THOMAS

Butter Cookies (chocolate-dipped)

I t is possible, in this day of ghastly treats marketed to children with names that include words such as "snax" and "froot," to whip up treats yourself that are very easy, very quick, and very delicious. This and each of the next four recipes use the following standard pantry ingredients.

ALWAYS HAVE ON HAND
flour
sugar
salt
eggs
unsalted butter
pure vanilla extract
semisweet chocolate chips
milk

These are so much better than Lorna Doones or Fudge Stripes, and they're a snap to prepare. You can even make the dough ahead of time, freeze it in a log, and just thaw, slice, and bake your cookies when you want them!

INGREDIENTS
2 sticks butter, softened
¾ cup sugar
2 egg yolks
1 teaspoon vanilla extract
2 cups plus 2 tablespoons flour
½ teaspoon salt
1 cup semisweet chocolate chips

1 Beat the butter with an electric mixer in a large bowl until pale and fluffy, about 5 minutes. Add the sugar and beat until the mixture is pale and very light, another 2 to 3 minutes. Add the egg yolks and vanilla. Mix until incorporated. Add the flour and salt and mix until a rough dough is formed.

2 Shape the dough into a log, wrap it in plastic wrap, and refrigerate for 2 hours (or up to three days).

3 Preheat the oven to 350°F. Slice the dough into rounds that are ¼ inch thick and place them 1 inch apart on ungreased cookie sheets. Bake about 14 minutes, or until lightly browned.

4 Melt the chocolate chips in the microwave on high power, stirring every 15 seconds. Dip the cooled butter cookies halfway into the melted chocolate and place on wax paper to cool.

YIELD 4 dozen cookies

Pound Cake (Chocolate-chip)

I t's important that all the ingredients are at room temperature when you start—otherwise, the batter will separate and the cake won't have that wonderful dense-but-light pound cake texture. You can warm up the eggs in a bowl of warm water and microwave the butter until it's soft if you don't have time to let them warm up on their own.

INGREDIENTS

1⅔ cups flour
½ teaspoon salt
2 sticks butter, softened
1½ cups sugar
5 eggs, room temperature
½ teaspoon vanilla extract
1 cup semisweet chocolate chips

1 Preheat the oven to 325°F. Grease and flour a 9 x 5 x 3-inch loaf pan.

2 Mix together the flour and salt. In a separate bowl, beat the butter with an electric mixer until smooth and creamy. Gradually add the sugar and beat until the butter is very fluffy, about 3 minutes. Add the eggs one at a time, mixing each one thoroughly before adding the next. Add the vanilla.

3 Mix in the flour in three parts and beat until the batter is well combined. Add the chocolate chips.

4 Pour the batter into the prepared pan and bake for 1 hour and 10 minutes. The top will be split and browned and a cake tester should come out clean. Cool completely before serving.

151

Gooey Brownies

These are chewy on the inside with a crackly crust on top—just the way brownies should be! Don't add nuts—those aren't safe for very young children. These are a great play date treat (especially when a mom stays for coffee, too).

INGREDIENTS

10 ounces semisweet chocolate chips (this is most of a 12-ounce bag, minus a couple handfuls for your "helpers!")
5 tablespoons butter
⅔ cup sugar
1 teaspoon vanilla extract
¼ teaspoon salt
2 eggs
½ cup flour

1 Preheat the oven to 350°F. Grease an 8-inch square baking pan.

2 Melt the chocolate with the butter and sugar in a heat-proof bowl set in a skillet of simmering water.

3 Remove the bowl from the skillet and stir in the vanilla and salt. Add the eggs one at a time. Stir in the flour and beat until the batter is smooth and glossy.

4 Scrape the batter into the pan. Bake for 20 minutes, or until the brownies just start to pull away from the pan. The center will still be gooey.

5 Cool completely on a rack and cut into sixteen squares.

YIELD: 16 brownies

221

Five-Minute Fudge Sauce

Pour this rich sauce over ice cream or cake, or use it as a dip for cookies! It's good warm or cold—and some moms might even save some just for themselves. We all love to have a snack once the kids are down for the night!

INGREDIENTS

10 ounces semisweet chocolate chips
¾ cup milk
2 tablespoons butter
½ teaspoon vanilla extract
pinch of salt

1 Melt the chocolate with the milk in a heatproof bowl set in a skillet of simmering water.

2 When the chocolate is melted and smooth, add the butter in four pieces.

3 Stir until melted.

4 Remove from the heat and add the vanilla and salt.

YIELD: about 2 cups

SUPER TIP

On a rainy day, put on the rain boots and raincoats, grab the umbrellas and go for a walk around the block. Kids think it's an adventure.

—ALEX, MOM OF NICHOLAS AND JULIANNA

Sweet Vanilla Popovers

Kids think popovers are a downright miracle, and this version is sweet enough to serve for a special breakfast (such as the first day of school) or a party treat.

INGREDIENTS

1 cup flour
⅓ cup sugar
½ teaspoon salt
2 eggs
1¼ cups milk
1 tablespoon butter, melted
1 teaspoon vanilla

1 Preheat the oven to 450°F. Grease a muffin pan.

2 Whisk together the flour, sugar, and salt. In another bowl, whisk together the eggs, milk, melted butter, and vanilla. Pour the liquid mixture over the flour mixture and fold until just blended. The batter may still have a few small lumps.

3 Fill the cups two-thirds full, and fill any empty cups one-third full with water so the pan doesn't burn. Bake for 15 minutes at 450°F, then turn the heat down to 350°F and bake for 20 minutes more, until the popovers are brown and crusty.

WARNING: Don't open the oven to check them until the last 5 minutes of cooking time or the popovers will deflate! When they're done, remove them from the oven, unmold them onto a rack, and puncture the sides with a sharp knife to let the steam escape. Serve immediately. These are great with butter and strawberry jam.

YIELD: 12 popovers

ACKNOWLEDGMENTS

Many thanks go to my friend and editor, Donna, for her confidence and encouragement, as well as her contributions. Also to my husband, Nick, for his love and for always seeing that the glass is half full, even when it looks empty to me. Much appreciation goes to Joan and everyone at Mom-mom's, who've taken loving care of my children so that I could write this book. Without their care and flexibility it could never have been accomplished. To my parents, Tom and Harriet, who showed me that hard work and commitment are always worthwhile; my sisters and brothers—Tommy, Kathy, David, Danny, Brian, Carolyn, and Jane—who have been many things to me over the years, from playmates to role models to friends; my mother- and father in-law, Jack and Nina, for their enthusiasm and generous support; Tim, for helping me with technical issues; and Kate, for moral support. I'd like to thank everyone who has contributed ideas for the book: Guy and Nafi, for their paper airplane testing; Trish, for her thoughts on how to entertain little boys; Lisa, for her whistle; Lauren, for her flowers; Jennifer, for the scoops; Carolyn, for the stilts; Deb, for her tip on singing and dancing; Vivian, for birthday breakfasts in bed; Lynn, for shoe tying; Linda, for her distraction tricks in the doctor's office and on the changing table; Beth, for bath and bed strategies; Tom, for Frisbee throwing; Max, for kick the can rules; Dan, for table football rules; Kathy and Dad, for canoeing tips; Carolyn for her photo and storage tips and painted tee shirts; Patricia, for the cardboard box buildings; Richard's teachers for the activity blocks and the milk carton boats; Chris, for the snow globes; Greg, for kite flying tips; Steve, for teaching me how to juggle; Donna, for her dress-up tips; Richard, Anita and John, for being "testers."